Ghostly Justice :
true accounts of ghosts pleading their cases in court

By

Dylan Clearfield

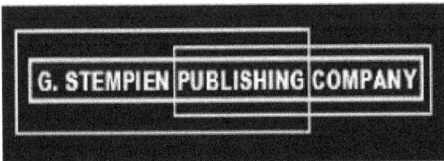

G. STEMPIEN PUBLISHING COMPANY

Published by
G. Stempien Publishing Company
All rights reserved

Editorial offices in New Quay, Cymru,

CONTENTS

OPENING STATEMENT

Do ghosts exist? Is the paranormal real? These are questions that humans have pondered for ages. And why not? If we could definitely answer these questions we will have a better idea of what's waiting for us "beyond the veil" to use a term more commonly heard in spiritualistic circles.

What is the best way to investigate these questions: do ghosts exist and is the paranormal real? Is legal examination the only or even the best way? In the 19th century - during the height of the spiritualist movement - renowned scientists such as Sir Oliver Lodge expended a great deal of time and energy rigging up seemingly foolproof tests for people who claimed to possess psychic powers. Could these people REALLY contact spirits? Many of the tests proved - or seemed to prove - that they could.

However, these eminent scientists were ignorant of the tricks that frauds and charlatans could play to fool even the most closely watching investigator. Once it was discovered that even the most clinical of test results could be compromised, none of the findings could be verified. There was always that doubt - that hint of chicanery.

The great illusionist and magician Harry Houdini understood this. He understood that most of the so-called incredible, supernatural feats of the psychics and mediums were nothing more than magic tricks - illusions. He dared them to perform their stunts in front of him. The few who accepted his challenge were exposed.

What then would be a better way to prove or disprove the existence of ghosts? If even modern day scientific testing isn't the answer - which it isn't - what is?

Most people already know the answer to this and have in fact suggested it. Bring the evidence either for or against ghosts before a court of law where it will be given an impartial hearing and a verdict based on logical legal principles will be rendered. Why not?

One of the major problems is getting something admitted into court as evidence. Evidence must be based on some type of proof either physical or circumstantial. For example: if you offer a picture of a ghost as evidence you would have to prove that any type of hoax could not have been possible. In this day and age of computer graphics that would be an impossible task.

Is it true, then, that if ALL the evidence pointing toward the reality of ghosts were taken to a court of law and presented as in any other normal case their existence would be proved by the preponderance of proof? Perhaps. But is this so-called evidence all that it is purported to be? Would the evidence that so many people claim exists really be admissible as evidence in a court of law? For something to be officially accepted as evidence it must undergo close examination and be verified beyond a reasonable doubt.

Return to the idea of using photographs of ghosts as evidence. Who could argue the validity of a photograph? It's something clearly visible right before your eyes. But so too are the greatest magic tricks.

There are folios filled with photographs of alleged ghosts. There are albums filled with so-called spirit photographs of deceased friends and relatives which have theoretically been identified as genuine by their closest loved ones - a phenomenon to be studied in depth later.

There are even movies of alleged ghosts. And tape recordings. But all of these related visual and audio products suffer from the same defect - potential fraud. None of the photographs or other videos and sound recordings could be accepted as evidence unless there was a trustworthy witness to the taking of the "evidence" aside from the person who was taking it. Even then it could be claimed that the witness was tricked.

Nonetheless, eye witnesses are crucially important to the

acceptance of evidence as being factual - be the evidence photographic, audible, textile or in any other form. And the more witnesses the better. And the more believable the witness the better.

One of the rarest of events is the sighting of a ghost by two or more people at the same time. AT THE SAME TIME! There have been many sightings of the same ghost by different people at different times, but extremely few sightings of the same ghost at the same time by more than one person. I have been investigating ghosts for decades and have access to thousands upon thousands of sightings from all across the world but have acquired only a handful of sightings of a ghost made by more than one person at the same place and at the same time. And the impact of such a sighting is profound!

Is there such profound evidence that would be admissible in a court of law as evidence? That's what we're going to search for in these pages.

Legal proceedings have been held concerning the supernatural. Ghosts have been called as witnesses and testimony from the grave has been elicited. Such legal proceedings are few in number, but they do exist. These are the matters that we will be studying, not psychics who've claimed to have helped police departments and not mediums who've supposedly solved crimes. This is a book about ghosts and how they have been directly involved in legal proceedings.

Most of the cases that will be before us are over one hundred years old. This doesn't make them outdated. It makes them precedents! Precedents are the legal guideposts from the past that modern jurists use to help them render a decision today.

The majority of information in this book was gleaned from official court records. Most of the additional sources are of a primary nature - in other words, not mere hearsay. What does the prevailing evidence say about the existence of ghosts? Let's begin the research with an unusual case from 1890 involving ghosts and the U.S. Postal Service

THE SPIRIT POSTMASTER

The first case to be reviewed was held in U.S. Federal Court. One of the main reasons for examining this case is to become familiar with a basic legal concept that was derived from it. This concept - called the provenance of human understanding - will be encountered time and again in future trials which makes this legal concept a precedent.

What this means is that during similar trials in the future

that involve ghosts and spirits the court will refer back to the findings in this case and use this decision upon which to base its own decision. Precedents are extremely important, particularly the one that was set in the following legal action.

The case of the spirit postmaster was held on April 5, 1890 in the district court of Michigan: UNITED STATES V. RIED. The proceedings were convened during the height of the spiritualist movement and concerned a man who claimed to be able to contact the other side through his own unique mail delivery system. As an aside - in addition to the main charge of fraud - the U.S. Postal Service also leveled other charges against the defendant, accusing him of interfering with postal authority. But that's another matter.

Doctor W.E. Ried referred to himself as the spirit postmaster because for a fee of between $1.00 and $5.00 per piece of mail he would deliver a message to the spirits and get a response. You can't get any more long distance than that! And reasonable rates - considering that distance! No wonder the U.S. Postal Service was suing him. How could they compete?

Although the spirit postmaster's basic rates seemed reasonable, the whopping $5.00 fee for his "special delivery" mail was quite expensive for 1890. Why were THESE deliveries so expensive? Because these envelopes to be delivered to the other

8

side had been either sewn closed or sealed with wax before being sent on their way which supposedly guaranteed against fraud.

The basic idea of Dr. Ried's services was this: for the proper fee he would deliver a letter given to him by a patron to a spirit of the patron's designation to whom a question would be asked or from whom advice would be sought. Theoretically, the spirit would receive the letter, steam it open - my assumption - read the question, answer it, re-seal the envelope, then place the original envelope in another envelope which would be returned to the spirit postmaster. Doctor Ried would then forward the envelope to his mail patron on this side of the veil. It isn't clear WHY a spirit would waste its precious ecto-plasm on a scheme like this, or where it would get the office supplies and the necessary stamps.

Doctor Ried had been in business for two years before being brought to trial. According to his attorney, the doctor had handled several thousand special deliveries between this and the other side with extraordinary success. In an effort to defeat the charge of fraud, the attorney was strenuous in pointing out how on many occasions Dr. Ried received a virtual return to sender from spirit addresses that had become vacant or which housed new spirit owners from the ones who had been there before. If the spirit postmaster truly were a fraud why would he tell his clients that he couldn't deliver these messages and lose the fee when it would have been just as easy to simply cheat the patron with a forged message of his own?

Return to sender, from a spirit on the other side! If a ghost cannot be located on the other side - where else could he possibly be?

The attorney's argument was not well accepted. Particularly when the prosecution pointed out that just before Dr. Ried went into the private postal business he'd sought out the aid of a convicted con artist to learn the "skill" of opening sealed envelopes without detection. The witness to this - the con artist who schooled the spirit postmaster - also noted how he taught Dr. Ried several other tricks of the trade as well.

Undaunted, the spirit postmaster's attorney challenged the prosecution to explain how – if his client's activities were fraudulent - he had successfully replied to thousands of questions that he had relayed to the spirits if not by supernatural intervention. This was especially significant when taking into account the highly personal nature of many of the questions which would've been beyond Dr. Ried's ability to answer on his own.

At this point, several of Dr. Ried's satisfied earthly clients were called to the stand to testify in his behalf. The prosecution maintained a continuing objection, stating that none of these witnesses could offer what legally would be termed competent testimony because - in regards to the answers from the other side - they simply believed what they wanted to believe. Ultimately, the judge agreed with the prosecution and did not allow the testimony of Dr. Ried's satisfied customers to stand.

The defense refused to give in. Doctor Ried's attorney requested that his client be allowed to demonstrate his abilities first-hand while under oath by contacting a spirit on the other side which would provide vindicating evidence. The judge denied this request. He ruled that this form of testimony would not be competent either because it involved a principle that was by its very nature beyond normal human understanding and would serve to confuse the jury, swaying it from making a common sense decision, and because whatever spirit that was contacted could not be proved to have specialized knowledge in any particular area. In addition, once a person was deceased he or she no longer had any standing before the law and for all intents and purposes did not exist. This concept would be refuted in later years.

In regard to the first argument against potential testimony provided by a spirit, the judge referred to a specific rule of law: PROVENANCE OF HUMAN UNDERSTANDING. This concept states: No man has a right to embark in a business, and insist that the legality of it be tested by principles beyond the understanding of others, and not by the apprehension of the courts and the juries of the country, if when tried and tested by common human understanding the purpose is found mischievous and unlawful. The jury is not to disregard its own convictions by reason of a cloud of mysteries which they cannot penetrate.

If that doesn't sound confusing, little else will. The judge's remark is almost as impenetrable as the occult argument attempted by the defense attorney. Basically what the judge said was that since the supernatural is by its very definition beyond the understanding of the everyday world, relying on it to provide a rational explanation for a specific phenomenon would not be admissible. It just plain wouldn't make sense!

Put another way: if testimony of a supernatural nature were allowed to be heard in this case its primary effect would be to confuse the jury and to distract it from the true facts of the case which was that Dr. Ried had learned the "skill" of secretly opening and then re-sealing envelopes from a con-artist just prior to embarking upon his spirit postal delivery service.

It was up to the jury to decide without any outside assistance what seemed more reasonable - that Dr. Ried secretly opened the envelopes, read the contents then answered them before re-sealing the envelopes, or that spirits on the other plane did it. Maybe matters wouldn't have been so clear if testimony was allowed from the other side. But could that testimony be trusted? That was another difficulty the judge had with that type of testimony: could it be trusted? He didn't think so. In the future, other judges would.

Insofar as the reality of ghosts is concerned, this case would rate as a no-decision. The judge was only ruling on the admissibility of the evidence, not its validity. Maybe a spirit on the other side could have answered questions in court, but even if so, the judge held that its testimony wouldn't be accepted. Why not? Primarily because of the Provenance of Human Understanding rule. The jury could not be asked to overrule its own common sense and good judgment in lieu of testimony from a source beyond its comprehension.

With this initial proceeding you get an idea as to some of the many entanglements of the legal system. This was a relatively uncomplicated case which became very complicated with the introduction of the supernatural.

This leads us directly to our second case, a murder case from the late 1970's whose outcome shocked the entire Chicagoland area. At the very center of this case is evidence provided directly by the ghost of the victim. (Information gained by this author first-hand from the major participants in this case).

13

ENTRANCED ON THE WITNESS STAND

Allan Showery was a young orderly who worked at a well known hospital in the Chicago area. Terisita Basa was a young, hard-working nurse at the same hospital. They were fated to come together one deadly evening in Terisita's apartment, during which the young nurse would be brutally murdered during a home invasion and robbery.

The death of the young nurse was mourned throughout the hospital - by everyone except the remorseless killer. Terisita's best friend Remibias Chua who worked as a respiratory therapist at the same hospital was particularly distraught Terisita and Ms. Chua were both Philippine and shared speaking Tagalog, a language native to the Philippines.

A couple of days after Terisita's murder, Remibias lay down to take a nap on one of the benches in her locker room at work. She was exhausted from her long schedule at the hospital. The locker room was empty at that time of day except for Remibias.

Remibias had only been asleep for a short while when a noise suddenly awoke her. Sitting up, Remibias was startled by the appearance of the ghost of her slain friend, Terisita. Before anything else could transpire, another employee entered the room and the ghost vanished. Only Remibias had seen the apparition.

From this moment onward Remibias began having recurring dreams about her slain friend. The dreams became not only more frequent, but became more and more detailed. Remibias saw the murder of Terisita played out before her in graphic violence. She saw how the young woman was battered about the head and neck and finally left to die near the bathroom sink, soaking in blood while pieces of jewelry were ripped from her lifeless fingers.

When Remibias awoke screaming from the nightmares, the ghost of the slain nurse more than once appeared to her and beseeched her to take the information that had been revealed to the district attorney in order to prosecute her murderer, Allan Showery. But Ms. Chua hesitated. She described the nightmares to her husband, a medical doctor, but he advised her not to tell the authorities because she did not really have any true evidence.

Finally, Terisita's ghost gave Remibias some evidence that no one else but the killer knew about. Terisita told her about a specific piece of jewelry that Showery had stolen from her at the time of the murder and had later given to his girlfriend as a gift. The ghost then provided Remibias contact information for relatives of the killer's girlfriend who could identify the stolen jewelry as once belonging to the deceased.

Now Remibias had important evidence to bring before the district attorney. She initially presented it to the Evanston, Illinois police and named Allan Showery as the murderer of her friend. The police were hesitant to take any action, probably assuming that Mrs. Chua was little more than a crank.

Remibias was determined, and got her evidence directly into the hands of the district attorney. Since the case had gone very cold very quickly the DA decided that he had nothing to lose. Following up on the leads provided by Remibias, the piece of jewelry that Showery had given to his girlfriend was located and later identified by the deceased's relatives as once belonging to Terisita.

Based on evidence provided by the ghost of the murdered woman, Allan Showery was arrested and put on trial for killing the young nurse.

The case went to trial at the Cook County Criminal Court Building in January 1979 before Judge Frank W. Sarbaro in Chicago, Illinois. The ghost of Terisita was going to take an active part in prosecuting her murderer. When her friend Remibias was called to the stand to testify as to how she gained access to the information that led to Showery's arrest, the spirit of Terisita took over the witness's body. Remibias fell into a trance in open court

16

and proceeded to relate exactly how the victim had been murdered.

The defense vehemently objected. After the testimony had been given, Judge Sarbaro called a recess and asked both sides to meet him in his chambers.

Here is where important reference is made to the ruling of the judge in the case of the spirit postmaster. Judge Sarbaro made essentially the same finding. He decided that the manner in which the evidence had been procured and the form in which Mrs. Chua had given her testimony - in a trance - was of such a disconcerting nature that it would be prejudicial to the case of the defendant. How could the jury be expected to render an impartial verdict when the supernatural played such a major role in the prosecution? The judge declared a mistrial.

Allan Showery was not released, however. For reasons known only to him, he chose to admit his guilt and confessed to the crime of murdering Terisita Basa. It could be assumed that he "saw the handwriting on the wall" in the testimony given by Ms. Chua while she was in a trance. By saving the state another murder trial, the defendant was rewarded with the very generous sentence of only fourteen years in prison.

What are we to make of the judge's decision in this case? Was it an affirmation of the reality of ghosts and the supernatural? No. Once again, the verdict of the court could at best be determined a no-decision. The judge did not rule in the positive about the existence of the supernatural evidence, just that offering it in open court would be a procedural error much like it would've been in the matter of the spirit postmaster - information that would have been presented as coming from sources unknown. The following interesting case recorded in England in 1922 is very much like the Terisita Basa case. It too involves a dream sent by a departed spirit in order to gain justice.

The spirits of the dead appear in many forms and in many ways to the living. One of the more common ways is through dreams - usually nightmares. It's as if some type of astral justice comes into play at times when no ordinary methods on the plane of the "living" can succeed. Supernatural inspiration is what is needed.

This type of dream being sent by the deceased to the living should not be confused with ordinary dreams - nightmares of the common variety - because they actually represent the haunting of a person's sleep much in the same sense that a building or location can be haunted.

ERIC TOMBE

This case concerns a young man named - appropriately enough - Eric Tombe. Mister Tombe was part-owner of a racing stable at Kenley, Surrey, England. His partner was a disreputable man named Earnest Dyer.

One day in 1922 Tombe, an ex-army officer, for reasons unknown had the back of his head blown off by his business partner. After the crime, Dyer took the body and dropped it into a cesspit on the stable grounds, then left town post haste.

Not long after Eric Tombe's murder, his mother - wife of the Reverend Gordon Tombe - began to receive frightful dreams in which the murder and disposal of her son's body were clearly depicted. She was shown his bloody, mangled body where it lay in the recess of a cesspit which was covered by a ponderous stone slab. Night after night she was plagued by this dream.

Neither Mr. nor Mrs. Tombe were aware of the existence of the racing stables of which their son had been part owner. There was not any earthly way that either of them could have known the site of the murder.

Succumbing to his wife's vehement exhortations, the Reverend Tombe undertook a search through available real estate documents and maps to find the stables that his wife had described to him, assuming them to be somewhere in England. He was shocked to come upon a location that exactly matched her description. The information was taken to the police.

Owing to the fact that Mr. Tombe was a parson, the police humored him and undertook the search he requested. Four cesspits were located on the grounds of the stable areas in question. After removing the heavy slab from the top of one of them the police found in the bottom of the pit the body of Eric Tombe just as his mother had foreseen.

The murderer - Earnest Dyer - had fled to Scarborough where he lived on money obtained from writing bad checks. He peered out his window one day to see the police approaching his home. They were coming to question him about a series of bad checks attributable to him. He thought that they were coming to arrest him for the murder of Eric Tombe.

Not wanting to take any chances, Dyer withdrew a revolver and blew out his own brains. The factual story ends there.

Once again, the spirit of the murdered person seeks and gets justice on its own terms. The series of events like these add up throughout this study of ghosts and the law. There is far more than simple coincidence involved.

The next case to be examined is in at least one way much

like the previous two. Although it does not involve a ghost, it has a strong supernatural element in it and features a person who could be transformed into a clairvoyant medium while under hypnosis.

A HYPNOTIC MEDIUM

The event occurred in Berlin, Germany in 1921. The wife of a shoemaker was found by the police dead in her bedroom. She had apparently been killed by strangulation as indicated by the bruises on her throat and breasts. Her husband was arrested for the crime but claimed innocence, stating that he was not at home at the time of the murder.

The post mortem examination of the deceased was inconclusive and the authorities were left completely baffled. Because there were not any clues by which to proceed - and certainly nothing incriminating against the husband - they had to release him, their only suspect.

In desperation the police commissioner called upon the assistance of a well-known hypnotist who had been consulted on such cases before. The hypnotist brought with him a subject whom in the past he would put under a trance which would effectively transform him into a clairvoyant medium. He would then become adept at taking readings from inanimate objects at the site of the crime.

The hypnotist and his assistant were taken to where the murder took place and were allowed to examine the scene, picking up any occult vibrations still lingering in the room. The hypnotist then placed his medium-subject into a trance and, while the subject held in his grasp articles that had at one time been used by the husband, he gave a vivid description of the murder.

The husband and the wife had violently argued on the night of the homicide. Enraged at one point, the husband grabbed the woman by the throat and flung her half unconscious onto the bed. After she fell, her head remained bent forward, eventually causing her to choke to death by blockage of the air passage to the throat.

After the subject had completed the description of the murder, he and the hypnotist were asked to leave the room for a few moments. The police commissioner wanted to perform a test to verify the validity of the trance-medium's powers. He proceeded to re-arrange some of the furniture and various sundry objects in the room where the woman had been killed.

Once this had been done, the commissioner summoned the medium back into the room and requested that he set up the furnishings and sundries exactly as they had been placed on the night of the murder. The medium did so without hesitation, putting back in their right places the objects that the police commissioner had moved. A comparison was made between the commissioner's drawing and the notes of the condition of the room on the night of the murder. The set up that the medium had arranged matched in every detail.

The husband of the slain woman was called back in for questioning. He was given an exact description of how his wife was murdered and was so shocked by the accuracy of the description and so appalled by what he'd done that he broke down and confessed to the crime.

When confronted with the evidence supplied by an occult force to the trance-medium how could the guilty person deny his act? It proves once again that even though the victims of criminal acts may no longer exist on this plane they still can in some way obtain justice through supernatural powers. Every detail of this bizarre case is factual.

TESTIMONY ACROSS THE GRAVE

Another story where the dead accuse the living was set underway on October 10, 1921 - the same year as the previous case. A seventeen-year-old high school student named Arline Stouts was murdered and found dead by her father. Her body was lying lifeless on the couch in her home, dressed only in a nightdress. Arline had suffered a bullet wound to her right shoulder, a wound that caused her death. At the student's side was an empty army revolver which her father had kept in a desk drawer in the hallway. It was now missing one cartridge. The death was originally classified as either a suicide or an accidental shooting but information from a ghost changed this finding.

A few days after the girl's funeral her distraught father went to the cemetery to be near his daughter. It was quiet and no one else was around. Suddenly, a specter appeared on the other side of the grave from the grieving father - a vision of his daughter. The information that she then gave him as she spoke over her own grave made it clear that her death was neither a suicide nor an accident; she'd been murdered and the spirit revealed who the killer was

Arline's ghost vanished. Her stunned father remained staring into the emptiness she'd left, trying to make sense of what he'd just seen and heard. It took him a couple of days before he regained his composure and he decided to go to the police station to tell them a story he wasn't sure they'd believe.

This is what he told the police verbatim: "I went to my daughter's grave on Saturday. While I stood there a vision appeared over the grave and Arline stood there. 'Father,' she told me, 'go to see Edwin. He can tell you all.'"

The Edwin spoken of by the ghost was twenty-one-year-old Charles Edwin King who had been the girl's boyfriend. The police had already questioned King who had declared his innocence, admitting only to having been with Arline on the afternoon before her death. He said that he'd left early that afternoon and spent the rest of the day in the nearby town of Bristol. King told authorities that he was still in Bristol when he'd heard of Arline's death.

Armed with the grave-side evidence given to them by Arline's father, the police looked more deeply into King's story and discovered that there wasn't anyone in Bristol who could account for his whereabouts during the time in question. A warrant was filed for his arrest and Mr. King was soon in custody for the murder of Arline Stout.

Once again a ghost had directly intervened to bring her own killer to justice. And once again, the type of ghost involved is not the usual type that we generally hear about or read about. They're not just figments appearing before windows. They can and do actively engage in contacting people on this side in order to bring about justice.

It seems pretty clear that there are various types of ghosts that occupy that shadowy realm between the living and the beyond. There is a particular classification of ghost which returns for the specific purpose of bringing about justice. In the upcoming pages we will see this type of ghost again and again. Why are these ghosts different from the "common" variety of ghost? An interesting question to ponder as we continue onward in our quest for the legal status of ghosts.

JESUS SENDS A GHOST BACK TO EARTH

The two men met in guarded secrecy. There could not be any witnesses to their dark meeting. The men were Guy Jack and Herbert Lipscomb, a medical M.D. Dr. Lipscomb was treating a man named C.T. Stewart who was very ill, but in his condition he might linger for years. Guy Jack had a plan that could gain a great deal of money for both himself and Dr. Lipscomb. Guy planned to take out a sizeable life insurance policy on Mr. Stewart but he needed the help of the doctor to make his scheme successful. Guy, a shrewd, devious businessman, wanted the doctor to find a way to speed up Mr. Stewart's demise. Then he and his accomplice would collect a large sum from the insurance company.

Doctor Lipscomb agreed to the scheme. The year was 1897, a time before insurance companies had large corps of fraud investigators - as they do today - or the database manipulation possibilities provided by computers. It was also a time when honest doctors worked more out of altruism than avarice and were

26

not multi-millionaires; and it was a time when malpractice suits were things of the distant future. Why did the doctor need the help of Guy Jack in this plot? Why not just kill his patient and collect on the insurance policy himself and not share any of the profits? Because it would've looked suspicious for a doctor to collect on an insurance policy of one of his own patients - wouldn't it? The two men needed each other in this dark conspiracy.

The scheme was soon set underway. Once the insurance policy was in hand, Dr. Lipscomb paid a visit to his patient, theoretically to check on his condition. He examined Mr. Stewart's vital signs and performed all the customary evaluations that a doctor performs. Then Doctor Lipscomb withdrew a special red capsule from his bag and gave it to Mr. Stewart, instructing him to swallow the pill. The obedient patient did as told. Assuring the household that there was nothing to worry about, the doctor departed.

Less than a half hour later Mr. Stewart fell into a convulsive fit. His wife and a servant raced into the bedroom while Mr. Stewart flailed in his last throes of agony. The following is a description of the scene as given in court:

Mrs. C.T. Stewart testified that her husband took a capsule about the time he went to bed and in about ten to fifteen minutes afterward he... "Threw up his arms, looking very wild about the eyes, and seemed to be cramped in great pain; then he had a convulsion and when he revived made the following statement: 'I am going to die. I have been dead and the Lord sent me back to tell you that Dr. Lipscomb poisoned me with the capsule that he gave me tonight. Guy Jack had my life insured and he hired Dr. Lipscomb to kill me;' then he had another convulsion and died."

At first, this testimony does not seem to make a lot of sense: "I am going to die. I have been dead..." And it is extremely important to understand PRECISELY what Mr. Stewart was saying at this point to be able to understand any of the rest of the statement. "I am going to die. I have been dead..."

What Mr. Stewart is saying - remember he WAS on his deathbed - is that he had ALREADY DIED and that he was going to die again - or return to that condition after giving them the message that the Lord had sent him back to give. This is crucial to understand.

Thus, when Mr. Stewart said, "I am going to die," what he meant was that he was going to die after making his statement. And what an incredible statement it was! "I have been dead, and the Lord sent me back...."

28

Why did the Lord send him back? To tell the witnesses in the room that Guy Jack and Dr. Lipscomb had entered into a conspiracy to kill him and that the capsule that the physician had given him was the murder instrument. Consider this: if Mr. Stewart had not truly been dead and at that time been given access to special information while there on the other side - no matter how briefly - how else could he possibly have known of the conspiracy between Guy Jack and the doctor? How!

Doctor Lipscomb was put on trial for murder. The statement made by Mr. Stewart was offered in evidence as a dying declaration - a statement made on one's deathbed which is normally accepted prima facie by the court, meaning that its validity would be automatically accepted. The corpse's statement was made voluntarily and without suggestion or undue influence.

Doctor Lipscomb was convicted of murder and sentenced to be hung. Here's where it gets even more interesting. Lipscomb's attorney appealed. He argued that the deathbed testimony was inadmissible in that the information supplied by Mr. Stewart came from a source beyond human understanding. Sound familiar?

It would not have been too unusual for the appellate court to have denied the appeal on grounds that deathbed statements are commonly accepted as evidence. There were certainly enough PRECEDENTS for such a ruling.

But the appellate court went one step farther - one great step! It made a point to rule that the ENTIRE STATEMENT made by Mr. Stewart would be accepted as admissible evidence in court. Why is this so important? Because incorporated in the statement was Mr. Stewart's remark that he had been dead but had been sent back by the Lord. It essentially was his ghost that made this statement because Mr. Stewart was already dead when he made it

Yes, it's a very confusing scenario. At this point, a person could rightfully ask: had Mr. Stewart really died and then come back, or had he simply revived for a moment, then lapsed back into death? The appellate court surely had to ponder this as well. It apparently concluded that he had died and the judges based this belief on the startling evidence that Stewart's ghost had produced about how and why he was murdered. How else could Mr. Stewart possibly have known about the scheme between Guy Jack and the doctor if not through the agency of some force beyond human comprehension? Coincidence would have been ridiculously impossible.

Ah, ha! But what about the rule prohibiting the acceptance of such testimony as admissible evidence? This rule applies to juries, not necessarily to judges. Remember, the decision under consideration right now was made by an appellate court which is comprised of justices, not a jury. It is assumed that a judge would not be so easily swayed by testimony that might normally be confounding to the average lay person. In addition to this, the appellate court rules on jurisdictional matters not necessarily on the evidence itself. Was proper procedure followed? Should Mr. Stewart's testimony be allowed to stand? In this case, the court decided it should! All of it.

The lower court's ruling was allowed to stand with an additional comment from the appellate court: that the entire statement made by Mr. Stewart would be accepted as evidence. Although not specifically saying so, the court ruled that Mr. Stewart's ghost had returned to offer testimony that could only have been acquired through supernatural means.

What of Dr. Lipscomb? His sentence to be executed was upheld, however he died in prison before the judgment could be carried out. There isn't any record of what became of his accomplice   Guy   Jack.

Murder cases aren't the only form of legal proceedings in which ghosts become actively involved. Also important to many of the deceased is the disposition of their worldly goods even after they have passed on to the other side. Although this sounds paradoxical - why would a ghost care about possessions he could no longer enjoy? - it actually makes sense because the spirit is primarily concerned with making sure that a relative or other loved one who is still alive receives the proper share of the inheritance as bequeathed.

THE GHOST WHO WAS LATE TO COURT

Sometimes a person draws up a will and forgets to tell the people it was intended for anything about it. This is the case with Jasper Barker. When Jasper Barker died at his home on December 13, 1864 from wounds received during a battle in the War Between the States no one in his family knew that he'd ever drawn up a will. Thus, his kinfolk simply remained on the land where they had lived with him and divided ownership upon his passing according to the order of their relationship to the deceased, unaware that Jasper had different intentions for his land.

Why hadn't Jasper told them about the will? Possibly because he hadn't expected to die from his wounds. Since he lived near the battlefield where he was wounded, he'd been sent home from the hospital with the intention of returning to his unit when healed. He never made it back to his unit.

For forty-five years after Jasper Barker's death his former land stayed in the possession of the members of his family just as they'd divided it upon his passing. Then all of a sudden Jasper's nephew - Jasper Craven - was paid a visit by his deceased uncle.

Although Jasper Craven was in an altered mental condition of some type at the time, the visitation of his late uncle wasn't really just a dream but more like a vision. It was a startling vision in which his uncle had an important secret to reveal to him. At this point, the court records will be opened to reveal the official abstract of the proceedings.

The appellee (Jasper Craven) is the oldest son of
Adeline Barker Craven and W. M. Craven and was born
on this land November 1863, and was named for his Uncle, Jasper.

Jasper Barker enlisted in the army with others of
the neighborhood, among which were Enoch Scotten
and F.M. York, both of whom lived near the Barkers.

Jasper Barker was wounded in battle and in September 1864, was in a hospital in Marietta, Geo. From here he was sent home on furlough. He died at his home on the land in controversy December 13, 1864. Enoch Scotten was also home on furlough when Jasper died and had visited him two or three times during his last illness.

After this, Scotten and York returned to that vicinity and lived there until 1879, when York returned to Kansas, where he died some years ago. Scotten continued to live in the neighborhood until 1909. The appellee lived with his mother, the appellant, until he was 24 years old or until 1877. Neither he nor Jane Barker the appellant had any knowledge of the existence of any will made by Jasper Barker until in the spring of 1909 when, as the appellee claims, his uncle Jasper appeared to him in a vision, or dream, and told him of the existence of a will and that it was in possession of Enoch Scotten who still lived in the neighbor-hood, and upon whom the request of the appellee produced and gave him the will.

This is according to the official court documents. So, to recap: the appellee was Jasper Craven, who was Jasper Barker's nephew, and the appellant was Jasper Craven's mother, Jane. Apparently Jasper and his mother did not get along very well because he was suing her for possession of the land on which both had been living.

The ghostly Jasper told the living Jasper that he'd left a will with Enoch Scotten about forty-five years ago, and Enoch was still living in the same home back then as now. Jasper paid a call on Enoch - who was quite elderly at this time - and asked him about the will. Enoch sauntered to an old chest, rummaged through it, and came up with the will, freely giving it to Jasper.

Two major questions come to mind: why did Jasper Barker's ghost wait forty-five years to contact his nephew about the will and if Mr. Scotten knew about the will's existence why didn't he tell anybody? Unfortunately, we'll probably never know the answer to these questions.

We can attempt an answer concerning the ghost's tardiness in bringing the will's existence to his nephew's attention. Maybe the spirit of Jasper Barker didn't become aware of dying until approximately forty-five years after he'd died. It's believed that when a person dies he is not always aware that he is dead and that some type of psychic shock must stun him into awareness of his altered condition. Maybe when Jasper Barker appeared to his nephew the ghost thought it was still 1864 and that he'd just died.

Remember, when Jasper Barker was sent home to recuperate he was expected to survive. His death would have been unexpected and as such may not have been realized by the spirit. It's possible that the spirit then wandered in timeless limbo for forty-four odd earth years until finally realizing the nature of its changed condition. Then the ghost of Jasper Barker appeared to his nephew.

Whatever the reason for the lengthy delay - the court

accepted the validity of the will and no one contested it. The court even accepted the reality of the ghostly visitant. The true legal problem for Jasper Craven, the nephew, was a matter of statute of limitations. The statute of limitations then for probating a will in Jasper's state was twenty years: if a will was not brought before the court within twenty years of its going into force it could not be acted upon. It would then be considered null and void.

But Jasper's attorney argued that the will had not come to light until 1909 - no one mentioned its existence until then. Therefore, the statute of limitations should begin running in 1909 not 1864 when the will was drawn up. So the main question is: when did the will become a valid instrument, in 1909 or in 1864?

The court decided - 1864. That was the date in which the will was drawn up before witnesses and that was the date of the death of the person who made up the will. The judge in the case made a very powerful comment which goes directly to our matter concerning ghosts and the law: "While it may have been the intention of the uncle to bestow upon the appellee the real estate of which he died possessed, yet if he had the power to appear to the nephew and disclose the existence of the will in 1909, he is the only one who can be said to blame, and his failure to make the facts known for 45 years had effectually barred the nephew's right to recover."

It was the ghost's fault! Officially and under the law. The judge stated that it was the procrastinating ghost itself which was to blame for the nephew's being barred from enforcing the will because the statute of limitations had run out.

Two other startling factual points glare out from this case: 1) the nephew DID RECEIVE some form of paranormal message concerning the existence of his late uncle's will, and, 2) it cannot be denied that the nephew suddenly knew where the will was and who had possession of it. Even the court accepted these facts. The validity of the will was never disputed, nor was the credibility of the only living witness to the drawing up of the will, Enoch Scotten. It was all the ghost's fault!

GHOST OF A BRITISH REVOLUTIONARY SOLDIER

The year is 1774. It is two years before the Declaration of Independence will be written and signed. However, British troops are already occupying certain locations in the American colonies.

We're going to examine a pre-Revolutionary ghost story of remarkable consequence. In fact, it is one of those extremely rare occasions when more than one person at the same time is witness to a supernatural event. But they don't see the ghost, they are witness to it another way.

The story begins in a British army camp. Two British officers are in their tent, awaiting the arrival of a fellow officer. Major Blomberg was the man for whom they were waiting. He had earlier taken a party out on a foraging expedition. It isn't clear what they were foraging for but it probably wasn't anything edible since his two compatriots were anxiously awaiting Officer Blomberg's return due to the special plans for dinner that they had already prepared.

It was with relief and expectation that they finally heard Major Blomberg's familiar FOOTSTEPS approach their tent. However, he did not enter but remained outside and spoke to the two men from where he stood with a voice that both of them plainly and without question recognized.

The major did not speak to his friends about the foraging expedition he'd just gone on or about the wonderful dinner plans they had. Instead he spoke about what seemed strange and out-of-place matters. He implored his two friends to do something very special for him when they returned to England.

Major Blomberg gave them specific directions to a particular house on a particular street in Westminster that he wanted them to visit. Once there, a search was to be made in one of the rooms - a room painstakingly described by the major - where they were to find a concealed box in which were placed some very important legal documents that would greatly benefit his young son.

After giving this message, Major Blomberg left the area - his departing footsteps as clear and familiar as had been his approaching footfalls.

The men inside the tent then leapt from their seats and burst out through the front opening in the canvas. They peered about them in anxious bewilderment, searching fruitlessly for Major Blomberg. He couldn't have walked out of sight so quickly!

The officers approached the nearby sentry and asked him what had become of Major Blomberg. The confused guard told them that he hadn't seen the major since he'd left on the foraging expedition.

The officers demanded to know if the guard had remained at his post the whole time. He swore that he had. This was particularly unsettling because if the sentry had been at his post as required it would have been impossible for Major Blomberg to appear outside the tent without having been observed.

The two officers went back inside their tent, greatly puzzled. Their puzzlement became shock when moments later a soldier requested admittance into their quarters to deliver some unfortunate news. Major Blomberg was dead! He'd been killed during the day's action while engaged in that fatal foraging expedition. His body had been brought back to the camp about ten minutes before, at the exact moment his ghost was speaking to them.

When their tour in America was up, the first thing that the two officers did was to make a visit to the house described by their fallen comrade. The household was of course distraught over the news of the major's death, even though it had been months before, and was somewhat perplexed by the two officers' request to search the room that had been specified by the major.

Following the directions precisely as given by Major Blomberg, they located the tin box he'd described to them and revealed the title deed to a valuable parcel of property in Yorkshire that had been bequeathed to the major's young son.

There had been bitter disputes among family members concerning the true heir to the Blomberg estate. By the intercession of Major Blomberg's ghost on that dark, dismal night in 1774 the legal question as to the true heir was settled. The major's son received the estate that was due him as his father had wished in this life and the next.

WHEN BROTHER GHOSTS SPEAK

The case that follows is confusing and somewhat complex. It is easier to understand if the simple basics are supplied first. One brother dies and his ghost appears to his living brother in order to explain to him how he wants his will handled. However, the second brother then also dies and his ghost appears to a close friend to explain to him how his and his late brother's wills are both to be handled.

This case comes from the same period of time as the previous one and took place in Maryland. It is a particularly interesting proceeding for several reasons. One reason is that one of the counsels at the trial that ensued was a former governor of the young state of Maryland named Robert Wright. A second reason is that the counsel for the defendants was Joseph H. Nicholson who later ascended to a judgeship in Maryland.

The events took place in Queen Anne's County and spanned the years 1791 through 1798. The United States had just passed its twentieth birthday, the aged John Adams was president, and courts of law in this country were still relying heavily for precedents set down in British courts. In fact, one of the precedents that was followed was the case that directly preceded this one.

The case at hand is centered mostly on the prime witness, William Briggs, and his numerous interactions with the ghost of Thomas Harris. Thomas Harris owned property in Queen Anne's County and had devised a will in which his brother, James Harris, was to be the sole executor. The will instructed James to sell the land upon Thomas's death and then to divide the money from the sale among Thomas's four children, all of whom were born out of wedlock. This is the only legal way that the children could inherit because if a will were not drawn up spelling out Thomas's intentions all of his worldly possessions would be turned over to his blood relatives in descending order of relationship to him.

One of the counsels in the case - Joseph Nicholson - took extensive notes of the entire affair and these give a very full account of the events. However, the notes are more analytical than intuitive, more descriptive than explanatory.

For example, this is Mr. Nicholson's summation of the affair:

It appears that Thomas Harris had made some alteration in the disposal of his property immediately previous to his death; and that the family disputed the will and raised up difficulties likely to be injurious to his children.

Pretty plain, but he forgot to mention the ghosts who were to become involved.

When Thomas died, his brother James sold the property in question but, rather than dividing the proceeds among Thomas's children, he kept the money for himself. James died without a will two years after his brother, Tom. The children of Thomas Harris then sued the estate of James Harris in an attempt to get ownership of the land that should have been theirs.

The ghost of Thomas Harris had already been making appearances to his old friend William Briggs before the death of James Harris. William Briggs was a Revolutionary War veteran - which ended less than two decades before - and had been a close comrade of Thomas's since boyhood. Instead of appearing to a complete stranger as seems common with ghosts in this predicament, the spirit of Thomas Harris had decided to contact one of his very best of friends.

The many and frequent appearances were later well-documented in the notes of Counsel Nicholson, presented here as written.

In March, 1791, about nine a.m., Briggs was riding a horse that belonged to Harris. In a lane adjoining the field where Harris was buried, the horse shied, looked into the field where the tomb was, and neighed very loud. Briggs now saw Harris coming through the field in his usual dress a blue coat. Harris vanished and the horse went on. As Briggs was ploughing in June, Harris walked by him for two hundred yards. A lad named Bailey, who came up, made no remark, nor did Briggs tell him about the hallucination. In August, after dark, Harris came and laid his arm on Briggs's shoulder. Briggs had already spoken to James Harris, 'brither to the corp,' about these and other related phenomena, a groan, a smack on the nose from a viewless hand and so forth.

Certain parties have claimed that the numerous ghost sightings were all part of a vast hoax perpetrated by William Briggs for some undefined reason. That accusation will be addressed from various standpoints shortly.

First - a more reflective, intuitive reading of this section of the attorney's notes. About nine o'clock one March morning William Briggs went riding down a country lane alone. When horse and rider came to a spot in the road that passed near the tomb where Thomas Harris was buried in the nearby field the horse became very agitated.

The horse stopped, peered horrified into the field, shied with alarm and neighed with wild excitement. Then Briggs saw the reason. His old friend Tom was walking toward them through the field wearing his familiar blue coat. This brief view was all that Briggs had before the ghost vanished.

The horse returned to normal and the steed resumed on its way.

It's well known and accepted that animals are sensitive to the paranormal, especially horses. One would expect that a horse would react strongly to the appearance of the ghost of its former master. That is precisely what happened. The record of the horse's reaction was clear. There is nothing in the notes to imply that William Briggs was having a hallucination. If he was...so was the horse!!!

Also of vital importance is WHERE the sighting occurred. The horse became agitated at the site of Harris's tomb, not at some other point along the road - but there! A coincidence? Not likely. Yes, horses ARE exceptionally attuned to the paranormal.

There's something very important about this field. The ghost of Thomas Harris is seen here repeatedly. This is critically important when it comes to examining the hoax theory. A person carrying out a hoax is not likely to pay attention to the finer details - the little things that keep recurring. Also, anyone perpetrating

THIS hoax would have to be highly knowledgeable about the supernatural based on the numerous "coincidences" that took place during the sighting of Thomas Harris's ghost during the ride by - the when, where and why of it that was just pointed out.

Let's examine some of these more closely. Once again looking at the attorney's notes, the interesting details will be underlined.

In October Briggs saw Harris, about twilight in the morning. Later, at eight o'clock in the morning, he was busy in the field with Bailey, aforesaid, when Harris passed and vanished: Bailey saw nothing. At half past nine the specter returned, and leaned on a railing: Briggs vainly tried to make Bailey see him.

This ghost certainly is active between eight and nine o'clock in the morning. It's also well known that spirits, for reasons yet unknown, seem to haunt certain locations at certain times. The spirit of Thomas Harris also has a penchant for leaning on things. So? These are recurring, consistent behaviors that it's doubtful a person engaging in a hoax would be attentive to.

Bailey himself at another time pointed out how desperately Briggs wanted him to see the ghost. Why would someone pretending to see something - which a person creating a hoax would be - be so earnest in his attempts to have another person see the same thing? This isn't human nature.

46

Resuming with the notes:

Briggs now crossed the fence, and walked some hundreds of yards with Harris, telling him that his will was still disputed. Harris bade Briggs to go to the aforesaid brother James, and remind him of a conversation they had had on the east side of the wheat-stacks on the day when Harris's fatal illness began.

So, the ghost is telling Briggs to remind the brother - James Harris - of a private conversation that the ghost, while still living, had once had with his brother James by the wheat-stacks. How could William Briggs possibly have known about the PRIVATE conversation if not having been told about it by the ghost while on his walk through the field with him that day in October? Isn't it possible that no such conversation ever took place and that Briggs just made it all up to make his hoax more believable? No. In an interview shortly before his own death, James Harris verified that such a conversation HAD taken place. However, of course, Briggs could have heard of the conversation by hearing of this particular interview.

William Briggs was questioned under oath about this conversation between the Harris brothers but refused to divulge the contents. The notes taken in court are very explicit about this.

The counsel was extremely anxious to hear from Mr. Briggs the whole of the conversation with the ghost, and on cross examination took every means, without effect, to obtain it. They represented to him, as a religious man, he was bound to disclose the whole truth. He appeared agitated when applied to, declaring nothing short of life should make him reveal the whole conversation, and, claiming the protection of the court, that he had declared all he knew relative to the case. Returning to the stroll through the wheat field that Briggs took with the ghost of Thomas Harris: Bailey was sworn, and deposed that Briggs had called his attention to Harris, whom he (Bailey) could not see, had climbed the fence, and walked for some distance apparently in deep conversation with some person. Witness saw no one. There does not appear to be any motive for fraud or deception in this case. The court didn't think so. The property was ordered to be divided equally among Thomas Harris's children, as he'd wished. Thus, the ghost of Thomas Harris had finally had its day in court - even though in a second-hand way.

There are many incidents in which departed spirits have attempted to continue advising loved ones in matters monetary even after they had passed on. Why? If the deceased person in question had held the position of financial advisor in one form or another while he was alive, it is to be expected that he would seek to continue in that role in his new existence. At least, that is the expectation in certain belief systems of the afterlife.

SPIRITUAL INVESTMENT ADVISOR

No matter WHY financial advice is given from beyond the grave, it is a fact of reality that spirits have provided it. This can be verified as a fact through various court records. One of the first examples is from a matter heard in 1901 in Dean v. Ross which was a very common type of proceeding from the times.

Mrs. Ross was a medium and Mrs. Dean was her client. Mrs. Ross had been holding regular "sittings" with the elderly widow in order to contact Mrs. Dean's departed husband. During one of these "sittings" the spirit of Mrs. Dean's husband allegedly advised her to transfer 15 security bonds worth a great deal of money into the medium's name. It seems pretty obvious that what this medium was "seeing" was her OWN future - in retirement.

Nonetheless, Mrs. Dean did as she was instructed and transferred the bonds. It isn't recorded why her husband's spirit might have wanted her to transfer the bonds to the medium or how it was supposed to benefit his widow.

However, after the passage of time and the commencement of a new marriage, the former Mrs. Dean got suspicious and sued the medium for return of the bonds. The subject matter of the case was relatively common because this type of swindle was being played on vulnerable elderly moneyed widows across the country by unscrupulous con-artists. These were the types of cheats who the great Harry Houdini was waging war against - quite successfully.

What made Dean v. Ross so remarkable was the commentary of the presiding judge. The following are his instructions to the jury:

If there was a message received from the husband, and the defendant (the medium) simply delivered the message, believing it to be true, to this plaintiff, why then that would not be any false statement with the reference to the transaction; that would be a true statement, and I meant you to understand that then the plaintiff (alleged swindled party) could not recover, if that was a fact and that was a real communication.

The judge is allowing the jury to determine whether it believed that the communication between the medium and the spirit of the dead husband had or had not actually occurred. If it had and the medium honestly believed that the message had really come from the late Mr. Dean then the instructions from the spirit to his wife to transfer the security bonds to the medium was proper and valid. The judge was ruling that the ghost of the late Mr. Dean could - both legally and actively - still give instructions on how his earthly possessions were to be distributed.

However, in this trial the jury believed that the accused had acted in a fraudulent manner and held that the transfer of bonds had been enacted illegally. This does not mean that the jury vetoed the existence of ghosts, just that in this one case the medium was a crook and probably made up the entire supposed conversation with the late Mr. Dean.

A GHOST LEADS A TREAURE HUNT

The next story we'll look into involves buried treasure, the occult, and the law. It is a very uncommon mixture and the story itself is another very confused and complex one, involving a man who claimed to be able to invoke the aid of ghosts to help him locate buried treasure. There is a common belief in the world of the paranormal that unusual lights often swirl above areas of ground where treasures are buried. The best time to see these lights is at night, of course.

Once again there are as many twists and turns in this case as in the most winding of labyrinths. It is quite entertaining and somewhat of a relief from the murders and atrocities of the more serious legal proceedings. This case was heard by the Court of Appeals of Texas.

A man named James Nurse represented himself as a

medium to one Mr. Alexander, stating that he could communicate with friendly spirits which assisted him in locating buried treasure. Mr. Nurse informed Mr. Alexander that upon psychic evaluation of his land he was certain that there was a large cache of money buried on the Alexanders' property.

For a fee of $20.00 Mr. Nurse would contact his spirit friends to discover the EXACT location of the hidden money. Mr. Nurse said that he would not collect the fee until after the money was found. Having nothing to lose, Mr. Alexander agreed.

At the time, Mr. Alexander was having construction work done around the foundation of his home. Prior to the meeting with Mr. Nurse, the psychic, some of the construction work had been completed. It was at this time that Mr. Alexander and his wife began to hear strange rapping noises coming from somewhere below the surface near his front door. The rapping steadily increased in frequency and volume. Eventually it was accompanied by weird ghostly moans and spectral lights dancing over the area of new construction.

This is approximately the time at which Mr. Nurse showed up on Alexander's doorstep with his treasure hunting scheme. Seems peculiar: was he DRAWN there by the spirits? Why should he appear - just now?

After Alexander agreed to the proposal, Mr. Nurse did a

survey of the property with the help of the spirits and determined that money was buried near where work had been done on the foundation. He was given the go ahead to dig there. Under the watchful eye of Will Mabry - the construction contractor - and Mr. Alexander, Jim Nurse took up a shovel and began to dig.

Mr. Nurse came up with $42.00 in cash! As strange as his finding of the money was, what he did with it was even more bizarre. He placed the money in a tin can, gave the can to Mrs. Alexander and instructed her to carry it to the back yard where Mr. Nurse re-buried it before the two witnesses. There was a reason for this. According to Mr. Nurse if the money had been handled any other way the spirits would have made it disappear and would not have told him where to locate an even larger sum of money. Seemed to make sense - sort of.

Sometime later that night, this same group of people returned to where the new foundation had been laid and Mr. Nurse dug in a slightly different spot from where the $42.00 had been unearthed. This time Mr. Nurse hauled out of the ground what appeared to be a bucketful of gold coins, a sample of which was taken from the top to show the witnesses. The spirit-assisted prospector then took his bucket of money to the front doorstep area and buried it there so that even more money would be found later. Mr. Alexander paid the $20.00 finder's fee as agreed upon and the digging for the day was concluded.

However, Mr. Nurse came back later that night to engage in some solitary prospecting for his own benefit. Remember the initial $42.00 that was found and then re-buried? It was still in the ground where Mr. Nurse had put it. But not for long: this is what he came back to dig up in the middle of the night.

When Mr. Nurse did not return the next day to do the additional digging for even larger sums of money Mr. Alexander became suspicious. He tracked down Mr. Nurse and took him to court, pressing the charge of swindling against him. The lower court convicted Mr. Nurse of swindling. However, the verdict was appealed and the case was re-heard by the appellate court.

In his oral plea in the appellate court, these are the exact words that Mr. Alexander told the judge: "I am not complaining because he got my $20.00 but I am complaining because he came back there and stole the money after he found it in the hole. If he will bring up that bucket of money that was dug out of the hole, I will dismiss the case. I will take chances on it being money. Jim Nurse did not deceive me, or misrepresent anything to me about money being buried in my yard, because the money was there, and he dug it up, and had it buried in the yard, so that he could come back that night and steal it."

The appellate court had a great deal to say about this case, much more than the lower court had. What follows are the exact remarks.

"We are of the opinion that the evidence does not support the conviction. If the appellant (Nurse) made the presentation that he was a spiritualist and could talk with spirits, this matter raised the question about which this court does not feel upon to discuss or decide. We read much and hear much about the question of Spiritualism and what it means, and about which the world may be more or less credulous or incredulous, and there is something in the New Testament to the effect that spirits shall be tried whether they are false or true."

And: "The alleged swindled party testified that he saw him dig up the money; $42.00 was found at one time; the amount found on the second night is not stated.

"It seems that the appellant was prosecuted by the state's witness because of the fact that he came subsequently and took the money - theft under the witness' theory of the matter. He found the money as he said he could; and the record is silent as to whether the discovery of the money was through the communication with spirits or not. Alexander was neither deceived or misled."

The appellate judges left open the possibility that Mr. Nurse may have had the help of ghosts and spirits in finding the buried money. That the money was found was a fact. Mister Nurse had fulfilled his part of the bargain and thus could not be convicted of swindling. That is why the appellate court overturned his conviction.

So how did Mr. Nurse know that there was money buried on Alexander's property and how did he know where to look? Did he really have the help of ghosts?

Consider: if he'd pre-buried the money which he later dug up what would be the point of it all? Mr. Nurse would have been "in the hole" by $22.00. Remember, the fee paid by Mr. Alexander was $20.00 and $42.00 was found at the first excavation site. If the $42.00 had been placed there by Mr. Nurse at some earlier time...? Do the subtraction.

The only answer that seems to make sense is the paranormal one. Mr. Nurse really did have contact with the spirits. He noticed the dancing ghost lights over the Alexander's property one night, knew what that signified, then asked for help from the spirits in locating the exact position of the buried money.

As an aside, Mr. Alexander did eventually dig up the so-called bucketful of gold coins. He told the court that he'd take the chance that the money was real. It wasn't. The only gold coins in the bucket were the ones on the very top that Mr. Nurse used to convince Alexander that he was genuine. The rest of the bucket was filled with old railroad washers. That leaves a person wondering about the honesty of Mr. Nurse, doesn't it? And honesty is the question when examining cases involving "mediums" and earthly possessions as in the next example.

Oil has always been a valuable commodity. What if a spirit promised to advise you on where to find oil? Would you invest in such a venture

HAUNTED OIL STOCKS

Mr. Burchill did invest in oil whose location was supposedly revealed by spirits. An acquaintance of his, Mr. Hermameyer, confided in him one day that he'd recently visited a spiritualist medium who'd obtained inside information from the other side. The spirits had informed the medium where a huge strike of oil was about to be made.

Burchill wished that he could share a part of the bonanza and he was told that he could. Shares of stock were available in an oil drilling company that was about to lay a well in the location that the spirit had pinpointed for the huge strike. Burchill bought ten thousand shares as quickly as he could.

When the gusher did not blow its top as prophesied Mr. Burchill blew his and sued Hermameyer to get his money back.

And this is what the judge told Burchill in language about as plain as the sludge at the bottom of a useless oil well: "...therefore, that the representations of the defendant (Mr. Hermameyer), if any, to the effect spirits had revealed, through a medium, in valuable quantities beneath the lands in question must, under the circumstances of the case, be regarded as insufficient to form a basis for relief to the plaintiff."

This is a translation of what the judge was saying: the information supplied by the medium could not be relied upon to be accurate and if you used this information on which to buy the shares of stock it was nothing less than a foolish mistake on your part, not fraud on the part of Mr. Hermameyer as you are trying to claim. In other words, Mr. Burchill had used very bad judgment in purchasing the stock and cannot blame anyone but himself for his mistake. Caveat emptor.

The judge was not saying that the medium was a fraud or fake, just that like in any other stock speculation her advice could not be trusted any more than another advisor's.

EVEN MORE GHOSTS FOUND AT HYDESVILLE

For those of you who know the history of modern spiritualism the name of Hydesville will be very familiar. This is the location where the Fox sisters first encountered the knocking ghost which caused so much furor first in the local community, then across the country and finally around the world.

It is surprising how few people - spiritualists and non-spiritualists alike - are aware of the verified haunting that occurred at this same location and was the subject of a then famous murder investigation.

It isn't necessary to recapitulate the entire history of the Fox girls' phenomenon. The focus will be upon the other haunting in the house which led to the murder inquiry.

Hydesville was a small farming community in the state of New York. The time was 1848. It was on March 31st of this year when strange rapping began to occur in the very modest home of the Fox family. Young Kate Fox established communication with an intelligent spirit by challenging it to respond whenever she snapped her fingers. It did as it was requested and modern spiritualism was born.

But WHO was this spirit? His identity seemed to have become lost in the overall story of Hydesville and spiritualism. During one of the rapping sessions - which were attended by a houseful of observers - the spirit gave his name as Charles B. Rosma, a traveling salesman in his previous life. The spirit informed the girl that he had been killed by the former owners of the Fox house while making a sales call. At the time he was thirty-one-years-old. He even gave the location of his secret burial - ten feet below ground in the cellar of the Fox's home. Armed with this information, excavation of the small cellar was begun. Most of the digging was done by David Fox, the older brother of the Fox girls, Kate and Margaret. When David reached the depth of five feet he came upon the remains of a suspicious wooden plank. He continued digging and a few feet deeper he uncovered shards of crockery and bits of charcoal. And a little deeper still were the telltale signs of a hasty burial - quicklime. The purpose of quicklime is to speed up the disintegration of a body. Not surprisingly, human remains were found immediately beneath the quicklime. Did they belong to Mr. Rosma the departed traveling salesman?

The identity of the deceased was the purpose of the inquest that was then held. The coroner called as a witness a young woman named Lucretia Pulver who had worked as housekeeper for the family who lived in the Fox home several years earlier. She recounted the night when a young salesman came to the house and who was eventually asked by the family to stay the night. When Lucretia had finished her work for the evening she was surprised to be informed that her services would not be needed again for three days. This was particularly odd since she usually performed the housecleaning on a daily basis.

Lucretia did as she was instructed and did not return to the house until three days later. When she returned she found a number of very disconcerting changes had been made around the house. Among them was something very strange about the cellar. In the center of the cellar floor there was now a large area of soft dirt which looked as if it was the site of recent digging. When she questioned her employer about this, Lucretia was told that these were the results of rats.

It was at this time period that weird noises began to come from the cellar. Rats? I think not. Ms. Pulver was still working there when the noises began. But very soon after the noises started, Lucretia's employers moved away and she lost her position as housekeeper. A family named the Weekmans moved in next, but did not stay very long because they were troubled by the bothersome rapping sounds. Finally the Fox family moved in.

Lucretia's former employer at the Fox house - a blacksmith by trade - was called to the stand. He said that he knew of the salesman in question but that he did not stay at their house. Nor did he recall the actual name of the salesman. The close-mouthed blacksmith denied any wrongdoing and said he could not account for any of the items that were found in the cellar floor during the excavation.

Additionally hampering the inquest was the inability to trace the earthly existence of Charles B. Rosma - the resident spirit of the Fox household. During one of the communications with the Fox sisters he'd claimed to be the father of five children, but none of their identities could be verified either. All of this turned out to be a matter of incorrect spellings. The rapping process of communication is extremely tedious and not always reliable.

However, the spirit could have rectified any misspellings. Why didn't he? Maybe the ghost was still in a state of shock after its sudden murder and was having difficulty recalling its past identity clearly. Maybe it was spelling its former name as best it could under the circumstances.

Another answer to the identity problem is that the spirit who contacted the Foxes gave out a false identity or wasn't truly the murder victim. If he wasn't the true murder victim it wouldn't matter to him if the crime were solved or not.

Not all spirits are honest. Not all spirits are good-intentioned. Maybe this particular spirit for reasons unknown was being purposefully misleading. What is significant, however, is that knowledge of the body in the cellar had been provided by the ghost. Otherwise, it may never have been discovered.

Unfortunately, without an identification of the body being made, the inquest was closed – unsolved

LEGALLY HAUNTED HOUSES

Before us now lay a great figurative neighborhood of allegedly haunted houses. Many of the allegedly haunted houses ended up in court as the subjects of legal proceedings. Many of the proceedings were held in the 19th century, and quite a few of them were in Europe. The tour will begin in France, take us to Britain, Ireland and then across the Atlantic to Canada and then to the most famous of all haunted house cases in the United States. Remember, all of the cases are real and all of them have been ruled on in an officially sitting court of law.

It's important to keep in mind the guidepost by which we are proceeding. Our search is for legally haunted houses, meaning habitations that a court or similar body has deemed by the law to be haunted. We are not looking for simply any old house that people claim to be haunted. That's what makes our search so difficult. IF legally haunted houses do exist, they are very rare. But do they exist?

BOLACRE V. PIQUET

The first case on our docket concerning haunted houses is a very old one, but a very important one, full of factual evidence. It occurred in France in the year 1550. A man named Giles Bolacre rented a house from a man named Pierre Piquet in a small town in the suburbs of Tours. Giles had a small family and for the first few days they all enjoyed possession of the nice, clean home. The rent was quite reasonable as well. Giles discovered why a few days after moving in.

Strange, ghostly noises started occurring at night, only at bedtime. The sounds became louder and louder and lasted longer and longer, until no one in the Bolacre family was able to get any sleep. Mr. Bolacre took his complaints to the landlord, but all that Mr. Piquet would say to him was that he owed payment until the end of the lease. There was nothing he could do about the annoying noises.

Giles Bolacre had no other recourse than to take his landlord to court. He filed a complaint with what was called the Parliament of Paris - these being the days before the French Revolution. In his complaint, Giles noted that his family was disturbed by "a noise and routing of invisible spirits, which suffered neither himself nor his family to sleep o'nights."

A trial was held from which only scanty information remains. However, it is known that Mr. Bolacre won his suit and had proved to the court's satisfaction that mischievous spirits were indeed keeping his family awake at nights. The lease was held to be null and void due to insupportable nuisances of the paranormal activity. Mr. Piquet was ordered to release his tenant from the lease.

However, because of a procedural technicality, the lower court's findings were vacated and a re-hearing was ordered. Realizing that he faced a formidable opponent, the landlord hired a well- known and very successful legal representative, Maitre Chopin to handle the appeal. Representing the tenant, however, was a man every bit as able, identified from records only as Monsieur Nau.

From the outset Mr. Chopin attempted to make a mockery of noisy spirits being a valid cause to void a lease, going so far as to admonish the judge who sat on the original case, stating that the jurist "had merely and mischievously encouraged superstition."

Mr. Chopin goes on to say that all such things as ghosts and spirits are figments in the minds of children and do not exist in reality. He then quoted several well-known personages who, according to him, shared the same opinion: people like Plato, Tertullian, Marcus Aurelius and Empedocles. Moreover, he added that if Mr. Bolacre's house was truly haunted he should seek the help of a clergyman rather than that of a judge in a civil court.

Mr. Chopin's equally versed opponent was well-prepared to counter his learned adversary's arguments. Mr. Nau duly noted, "As to Plato, cited by my learned brother, Plato believed in hauntings, as we read in the Phaedo." He then observed how the Romans accepted the concept of ghosts and other spirits - otherwise, why have a specialized formula for exorcizing them? Next, Mr. Nau cited Pliny, Plutarch and Suetonius as other examples of men possessing uncommon intelligence from ancient Greece and Rome who supported the belief in and existence of ghosts.

After all, he shrewdly pointed out, it was necessary to actually tear down and demolish the accursed residence of the depraved Emperor Caligula to drive away the ghost that had haunted it for so long. In addition, he noted that even the early church Fathers were known to be believers in ghosts. After all, weren't ghosts supposed to be spirits released from Purgatory to make amends on earth for some misdeed?

Finally, Mr. Nau concluded by saying, "The defendant has let a house as habitable, well knowing the same to be infested by spirits."

The judges took the matter under consideration. None of

the particulars of the case itself had changed - there had only been more rhetoric in the hearing of the appeal - so the decision of the lower court was upheld. Letters Royal (official documents) were obtained for the tenant and the lease was voided without further chance for appeal.

In these proceedings, the court had officially ruled that the house that had been rented to Mr. Bolacre was sufficiently proved to be haunted by ghosts. Since the tenant did not know of this condition when he entered into the lease agreement, he could not be forced to remain. The house was deemed legally haunted and Mr. Bolacre was free to locate another residence!

A FIERCE POLTERGEIST

We remain in France for our next case and jump ahead forty-five years in time to the year 1595 - still well before the days of the French Revolution. This proceeding is very similar to the first one and takes place in Bordeaux.

Once again a distraught tenant was seeking the cancellation of his lease due to an infestation of ghosts. Once again, the landlord hired an attorney with a great talent for oratory. He used sarcasm as his primary verbal weapon. Following is an abstract of the argument he put before the court.

"The only apparitions in the world are the good or evil designs of the soul suggesting good or evil thoughts;" that "as to the supernatural, the ancient bacchantes and priestesses of Cybele fancied they were inspired, when in fact they were only tipsy with the fumes of wines;" and, second, that "even assuming the presence of demons, the complainant had not shown that before his departure he had used diligence to drive them away;" that "he had not resorted to lawping feathers, nor to the gall of the dog," that "Saint Chrysostom says that devils cannot infest a room wherein is kept a volume of the Holy Scriptures."

Thus, according to the attorney it was the tenant's negligence in not exorcising the offending spirits that was the problem, not the offending spirits themselves. Apparently they had a right to be there, according to him. Also, he was implying that the tenant was something less than a good Christian since if he had been he surely would've had a copy of the Holy Scriptures prominent in his home, which in itself would have warded off ghosts and demons. At least, that was the attorney's argument.

The court took all of this under advisement. To settle the matter, the court appointed a group of commissioners to visit the home of the alleged haunting and to return with its findings. Sometime later, the commissioners returned and reported to the court that none of its members could discern any form of haunting.

Acting on the report from the commission, the court rendered a verdict in favor of the landlord and ordered that the terms of the lease be enforced as originally agreed upon.

ANOTHER FIERCE POLTERGEIST

The tenant involved in another French case which was heard in 1860 fared somewhat better. The tenant was Monsieur Lesage and he lived in a house on the Rue des Noyers which had become well known in the district due to the violence and intensity of the spectral attacks on the poor man's home. Many of his neighbors and friends were first-hand witnesses to the paranormal activity, having been inside the house when the ill-spirited ghost unleashed its wrath.

It was an angry ghost which wantonly hurled all types of objects about the house, having little care who was injured in the process. And many people had been injured because the assaults would begin all of a sudden and stop just as abruptly. Huge chunks of coal and large logs of half-burned wood were some of the objects that were cast about the house.

But what made the attacks even more dangerous to Monsieur Lesage and any visitors was that many of the items heaved through the air were invisible. People would be hammered by great, heavy pieces of they-knew-not-what and found themselves battered to the floor or slammed against the wall. Some people were rendered unconscious and others required medical attention. Soon no one dare set foot in Monsieur Lesage's home on the Rue des Noyers.

The tenant took his grievance to court and sought to have his lease canceled due to the furious ghostly activity. Upon hearing his complaint, the court acted in a similar manner to the previous case and dispatched a bailiff from the local police to investigate the matter. A man named Vaillant was sent to the infamous house to gather information.

Moments after Vaillant stepped inside through the doorway, a gigantic block of coal crashed through one of the windows, slammed into a wall and shattered into many small fragments. The bailiff just barely missed having had his head crushed against the wall by the boulder of coal.

Vaillant did not need any more evidence. He promptly returned to the police station, filled out his report, and delivered it to the court. The verdict of the court was that the house was legally haunted by nefarious spirits and that the lease between Monsieur Lesage and his landlord was deemed null and void. Lesage was free to find another, safer, place to live.

A VERY INTELLIGENT POLTERGEIST

The next case that took place in France is slightly different in that it involved a libel case rather than a matter of breaking or upholding a lease, as most of the haunted house proceedings usually center around. It took place in Paris in 1849. What transpired was fully reported in the *Gazette Des Tribunaux* of February 2, 1849.

While demolition was under way to construct a new street that was to join the Sorbonne to the Pantheon and the Law School, laborers came upon an old house that was placed in the middle of a coal and lumber yard. The house was only one story high and had an attic.

Living alone in the small structure on the Rue des Gres was a miserable, though wealthy, old miser named Monsieur Lerible. For reasons yet to be determined, this little house in the middle of a coal field/lumber yard was subject to vicious assaults from an unknown source when dusk approached. It was as if the evil side of Nature Herself were angry with the miser who lived there.

Just as twilight would be falling, so too, it seemed, would be the sky. Projectiles that consisted mainly of building materials like paving stones, moldings and chunks of slate flew at the house from all directions. The tiny, lonely building seemed to cringe with fear as the walls were battered and the windows were shattered. The owner tried prevent the attacks by closing the shutters but only to discover that some elemental force flipped the slate projectiles onto their sides so that they would fit through the slits in the shutters edgewise.

By the time that the house was located by the laborers who were working on the new street the assaults had been taking place for three weeks. The workmen alerted the local gendarmes about the situation and, unknown to the occupant of the house, the local inspector of the police and several reliable observers took up posts on nearby rooftops and other elevated locations in order to witness the peculiar bombardment.

Dusk came and so did the attack. Projectiles of building materials descended from the clear sky from all directions, directed with uncanny accuracy at the beleaguered target. There wasn't any specific location from which the bombardment was unleashed, nor was there any human agency involved. For that matter, neither was there any natural cause that could account for the deluge of building materials on the little house.

The local newspaper the *Le Droit* began covering the story. Its publisher, Monsieur Francois, had an idea as to the origins of the attack. Maybe the owner of the house, the rich coal merchant Monsieur Lerible, was causing it all himself. This remark by the publisher of the *Le Droit* incense Lerible!

Enraged by the implication that he himself was the cause of the disturbances around his property, the landowner filed a libel suit in court against the publisher of the *Le Droit*. Monsieur Lerible also made a lengthy statement to the Marquis de Mireville who included it in his book, "Spirits and Their Vicious Manifestations."

Following is a portion of what the coal merchant had to say - a man of many words when he chose to use them. "Would you believe it, that they had the nerve to accuse me of all this - me, the owner, who has been more than thirty times to the police to ask them to deliver me, who on the 29th of January went to the Colonel of the Twenty-fourth, who sent to me a platoon of his Chasseurs? And another thing: suppose it was I who demolished myself. Should I have furnished the house with new furniture, as I did a month before? Should I have had all my furniture spoilt, like the sideboard with mirrors, which the stones seemed aimed at?"

Good questions. Why would a man who'd just newly furnished his home destroy the furnishings? Not only why - but how! How could Monsieur Lerible heave massive chunks of building material on his own house from an indefinite location in free space a hundred or more meters in the air? How could anyone? Anyone human that is.

This clearly seems to be a case involving poltergeist activity. That is the best explanation which makes sense. Not only does the modus operandi fit the workings of a poltergeist, but a cause can be determined. It doesn't seem a coincidence that the bombardment of Monsieur Lerible's home started at the same time that construction was begun on the new road being built in its vicinity, stirring up some ancient demonic spirits who'd been at rest. Or perhaps an old cemetery had been disturbed. SOMETHING was disturbed by the new construction, something not benevolent!

What is the final conclusion in this matter? The central question in this case is a matter of libel. Was *Le Droit* legally negligent by accusing Monsieur Lerible as being liable for the destruction to his own property? And if the newspaper was at fault, how should the matter as a whole be resolved?

The courts agreed with the landowner; the newspaper had made a libelous statement against him, for which it had to pay a fine. Since the property owner was found innocent of the damage done to his property and no other human agency could be held liable, the court concluded that the destruction had been caused by ghostly phenomenon.

This concludes our tour of the legally haunted homes of France. We've seen two instances where a renter was driven from his abode by the actions of hostile ghostly entities, and one case in which the victim was the homeowner himself who was also victimized by a libelous remark in local newspaper. In two instances, the courts decided that there was proof of a ghostly agency at work.

From France we'll turn our attention to courts that follow a British form of jurisprudence and that have a close relationship to the American legal system. In fact, the American system was based on the British and in the early days of our Republic - before we had our own legal history to look back to for precedents - we relied on British past decisions for our guideposts. This being so, we'll begin in England.

Although England is one of the most haunted countries in the world, it boasts very few legally haunted houses. Remember, a legally haunted location is rare. It's not just any old place that has a reputation for spooks; it has to have been adjudged haunted by a court of law.

ELFIN GHOSTS IN THE CORNERS

This case from the English countryside also involves a question of libel. The year was 1903 and the main participants in this story are Stephen Phillips and his young daughter. It's a very simple story and in some ways a quaint story, like a still life from another, simpler era.

Stephen Phillips was born on July 28, 1864 in Summertown, Oxfordshire, England and was educated at Trinity College, Stratford-Upon-Avon, and King's College. These are certainly very impressive credentials.

Stephen had always had an interest in drama and in 1885, at the age of twenty-one, he began a brief career as an actor with the F.R. Benson Acting Company. Discovering that his true talent was in writing rather than acting, Mr. Phillips created his first plays at this time. It was in 1900 that he wrote his most famous piece called, "Paolo and Francesca," a Shakespeare like romantic drama. In fact, it was so well received that he was favored with comparison to THE William Shakespeare - or Francis Bacon, depending on whose theory one accepts as to the true author of the plays in question.

Paolo and Francesca was a huge success. Mister Phillips made more money than he'd ever made before. It was time to move out of his cramped and noisy flat and find a quiet place in the English countryside where he could write in peace and his young daughter could have room to play in the fresh air. Besides, the death of his wife had left bad memories in the former home and Stephen and his daughter needed a change.

They found what seemed to be a quiet little cottage and rented it. Stephen was not yet forty and had hopes of a successful writing career and his daughter looked forward to meeting new playmates. Neither of them expected what was about to happen.

It wasn't long after moving into the countryside cottage that it became clear that something was wrong. It became clear in the strange, sudden reactions of the servants to sounds that came from nowhere and in the shadowy images that appeared without warning to startle everyone. It became clear in the uneasiness of the family pet. Something from another realm was occupying this cottage

The random noises didn't have any pattern or seeming purpose to them. A knock on a bedroom wall. A rapping on a table. A creaking of the stairs when no one was there. There wasn't any intention to communicate - just a demonstrated presence.

Time and again Mr. Phillips would be disturbed in his writing when the study door opened and closed on its own. The peace that he and his daughter had sought in this country estate was violated daily.

Even more distressing was what Mr. Phillips' daughter was seeing. On many occasions she glimpsed tiny, elf-like creatures scurrying rapidly across the floor to disappear in the shadows of the corners. When anyone rushed to search the corners or directed light into them there was never anything to be seen.

The appearance of the elf-like beings was particularly troubling. In parapsychology this type of apparition often represents the psyche of a deceased loved one, usually either of a spouse or a parent. The figure itself could either be the true spectral appearance in the after-life of the deceased person in an altered form or it could be the mental creation of the deceased person by the surviving loved one - an oddly distorted mental picture.

In other words, the elf-like creatures could either have been the late Mrs. Phillips' true astral form projected from the other side or it was the psychic depiction of her that had been developed by the mind of either her former husband or her daughter or both. In any event, it was much more than a mere coincidence that this type of apparition appeared here.

The strange noises continued. The study door opened and closed by itself. The elf-like beings continued to skitter about the house.

It was not long before Mr. Phillips and his daughter departed the unquiet house. At the time, Stephen Phillips was a celebrity and his sudden departure was considered newsworthy. The story was run in the local newspaper, including an in depth description of the ghostly happenings.

The owner of the cottage was very upset at the release of such a story. Renting a haunted cottage would not be easy. And it wasn't.

The landlord sued the newspaper, requesting damages and charging libel. He argued that the story of ghostly appearances at the cottage had greatly diminished the value of the property.

The court agreed. An award for damages of 90 pounds was given to the landlord.

Did the court rule that the cottage was legally haunted? Not directly. But the court did rule that a haunted house would be worth less in value due to the presence of ghosts.

Cases where tenants move out due to ghostly manifestations and then sue to break the lease and have a requested amount of money returned to them are one of the more common forms of haunted house proceedings. Next prominent are cases where libel is involved in which either a person or a property are defamed because of an alleged ghostly presence. Extremely rare is the type of case which is next on the docket, concerning the blustery Captain Molesworth.

THE CAPTAIN ATTACKS THE GHOSTS

Captain Molesworth - retired - was a former officer in one of Her Majesty's more famous regiments. He was a man of little humor and strong discipline. The captain was not easily intimidated, not even by ghosts or any other beings from the other side.

Upon returning to Scotland after being abroad in the service of his country, Captain Molesworth settled with his small family in a quaint village named Trinity which was only a couple of kilometers outside of Edinburgh. He rented a large town home from Mr. Webster, who was also his adjoining next door neighbor.

The Molesworth's had not even fully unpacked before the first indication of trouble of a ghostly nature began. At first, as is common in such cases, the problem came in the form of banging and rapping on walls, floorboards and other portions of the home. The noises quickly became insistent and very annoying.

For reasons difficult to understand, the captain initially suspected that the noises - which obviously weren't typical household noises - were being made by his landlord next door, Mr. Webster. It wasn't clear WHY Mr. Webster would make such racket. Why drive out a tenant to whom the property had just been leased? But that was the captain's belief. So, he began punching and boring holes into his adjoining neighbor's walls in an attempt to discourage the ghosts and drive them out.

When it became clear that Mr. Webster was not the culprit, Captain Molesworth became determined to find out who was. And Captain Molesworth was a VERY determined man - almost to the point of being psychopathically driven. He began searching for the noisy demons by tearing up floorboards when it seemed that the bothersome sounds were coming from underfoot. When this didn't work, he took to tearing out the baseboards whenever a strange knocking or rapping seemed to be coming from there. No luck with that tactic either, but he was at least working his way around the house.

The noises got louder and the military man got more determined. He finally loaded one of his muskets and fired several rounds into the wainscoting to force out the noisy spirits. This action seemed only to drive them even deeper into the wainscoting, while continuing their racket.

Not only was this the case, but now the spirit or spirits began to attempt some form of communication. Maybe it was a plea to stop the attacks being waged by Captain Molesworth. Familiar tunes of the day were tapped out. When the originator of the rapping was asked a question that required a numerical answer - such as the sum of ten and two - it would knock out the correct number.

Remembering that this took place in 1835, it should be noted that it occurred well before the supposed birth of modern spiritualism in 1848. Importantly, there were also two adolescent females associated with the Molesworth household as was the case with the Fox sisters in Hydesville. However, one of the Molesworth girls - Matilda - had died not long before these events had begun. Matilda's living sister Jane was a bedridden invalid.

Add the ingredient of the military strictness of this household and it's clear that conditions were ripe for a poltergeist outbreak. Maybe the captain was looking for the source of the rapping and knocking in the wrong place. Maybe he should've been looking to his own children - both of them. Could the disturbances have been Matilda's way of attempting to contact her bedridden sister?

Apparently the captain did not even consider this idea – yet! His next step was to contact a military unit which was stationed at the nearby town of Leith and request some of the soldiers stand guard outside his home to check for ghostly intruders. He also requested assistance from local freemasons and sheriff's deputies. His house was placed under close guard from all directions. Nothing unusual was ever located outside the house. But inside, the rapping, knocking and elementary forms of spirit communication continued.

Despite all of the measures taken by the captain, he never did discover the source of the noise-making. Exasperated, the defeated military man retreated from the house with his family. The landlord then took him to court. He didn't sue for past rents or for breaking the lease. He sued because of the damage that had been done to the property by Captain Molesworth's vigorous ghost hunting. In addition to this he lodged a libel suit, claiming that the reputation of the property had been ruined by the insinuation that it was haunted.

The case went through two hearings and extended over two years. The court decided against the landlord in the first hearing, but on the appeal the verdict was partially upheld and partially overturned. The appellate court ruled against the libel charge - since the house had been already let to another tenant - but did grant damages to the landlord for the destruction that had been done to the property.

What of the ghosts? No true history of a haunting was ever associated with this house. It seems highly likely that the ghostly phenomenon that occurred here during the Molesworth residence was the result of poltergeist activity centered upon the two girls - the bedridden Jane and her departed sister, Matilda. One can only wonder how the Molesworth's fared at their new residence.

THE DISEMBODIED HAND

Mister Waldron - a lawyer's clerk by occupation - lived in Dublin, Ireland with his wife. In 1885 their house came under attack from unknown forces. Mr. Waldron's solution was to sue his next door neighbor, Mr. Kiernan. The suit is reminiscent of Captain Molesworth's action also taken against his next door neighbor in which there also wasn't any evidence against the accused. It seems that the adage might be: when it doubt, sue your next door neighbor.

While it was true that the Waldron's home had sustained damage and was under some form of attack, there wasn't anything to point toward Mr. Kiernan as being the culprit other than his proximity.

Even evidence presented in court BY THE COMPLAINANT'S OWN WIFE - Mrs. Waldron - directed guilt away from Mr. Kiernan.   According to her testimony, on one terrifying occasion she witnessed a spectral hand use a glasscutter to slice a hole in a window pane in the sitting room through which it reached inside. Mrs. Waldron could think of nothing else to do but to locate the nearest handy weapon - a pair of tailor's shears - to hack at the intruding hand. She succeeded in lopping off one of the ghostly fingers. At this point, the remainder of the hand was

84

withdrawn through the window and vanished.

The local constable was immediately summoned to the scene. A thorough search was made of the area of the finger-hacking but no sign of the finger or of any blood could be found. There wasn't any trace to be found on the shears, either.

This event could not be blamed on the next door neighbor who, being a mate in the merchant's service, was not even in the country at the time of the incident. But something did happen and Mrs. Waldron was terrified. And an official police report had been filed.

What was attacking the Waldron home with such vehemence? More than twenty witnesses were called to the stand in the ensuing trial and swore under oath that from August 1884 to January of 1885 they observed stones being hurled by an unseen force through the windows and at the doors of the Waldron house. More than twenty people swore to this!

Again, this did not advance Mr. Waldron's case against Mr. Kiernan because none of the witnesses could identify any specific perpetrator. Neither did the testimony of Waldron's maid who told of numerous occasions where she'd been so frightened by the sound of disembodied footsteps and thunderous bashing sounds from the upstairs rooms while she was home alone that she summoned the police. The police reports from the Waldron home had begun to stack up on the constable's desk.

Under vigorous cross-examination by the complainant's attorney none of the witnesses changed their testimony. They had seen and heard the violent attacks on the Waldron house, but none of them saw the accused - Mr. Kiernan - at the scene of any of them.

It's difficult to understand why Mr. Waldron persisted in his suit against his neighbor since there wasn't any evidence pointing to him. Most likely, he was trying to find someone living on this plane of existence to blame for the damage that had been done to his house in order to get someone to pay for the damages. Mister Waldron certainly couldn't collect damages from ghosts.

Unfortunately for Mr. Waldron, that was what he was going to have to do. Upon hearing all of the evidence, the jury found Mr. Kiernan innocent of any crime and found that ghostly presences were the cause of the damage done to his home. Thus - another verdict directly naming ghosts as the culprits and classifying this as a legally haunted house.

WICKED SPIRITS ASSAULT A FAMILY

A very similar case occurred just five years later in the Irish village of Drogheda which is located but fifty miles north of

Dublin. It seems strange that two cases as rare as these should occur within fifty miles of each other AND only five years apart! But, then again, aren't ghost sightings by their very nature strange? The next case is a little more gruesome, however.

The besieged cottage in question was rented to a tailor and his family for 23£ a year in a small village of modest households. The first paranormal event occurred only a couple of weeks after the new tenants moved in. Just as the husband and his wife were about to retire to bed for the night, a phantasm foot kicked the candlestick from their nightstand. While they were still staring at each other in shock, the figure of a ghostly woman dressed in white appeared in the bedroom doorway. She hurled an object of unknown type at the tailor's wife which vanished after it had struck her. Then the specter followed suit and also vanished.

At the same time, horrific noises poured from the bedroom upstairs where the children slept with their nurse. The parents sprang from bed and rushed to their children's room. They were shocked by what they found inside. Furniture was smashed and broken, floorboards had been torn up and the children were lying half in and half out of bed giving every indication of having been badly beaten.

The nurse was gone. It was discovered days later that she had fled the house from whatever monster had attacked. The tailor and his wife were terrified for the well-being of their children. Their children were understandably traumatized and did not want to remain in the house.

The tailor sought legal advice and was told that he should not pay any rent that was due and to file in court to have the lease voided. This is what he did. The landlady, on the other hand, not only refused to allow him to break the lease, she demanded pre-payment of a quarter of the year's rent.

A double suit was filed in court: the landlady suing for back payment of rent and the tailor suing for vacating of the lease. The case was heard before a Judge Kisby.

The tailor's attorney presented the facts of the case, then he requested to summon several witnesses to the stand. The judge refused.

For her part, the landlady said that whether or not the house had been haunted was a matter that was not discussed beforehand so, according to her, it was a simple matter of caveat emptor - let the buyer (renter) beware. The tailor was unaware that the house he'd leased did have a long history of being haunted and that previous tenants had bitterly complained about the residence being uninhabitable due to the ghostly infestation.

Despite all of the factual evidence, Judge Kisby ruled against the tailor and his family, ordering the full term of the lease to be paid whether or not the tenants chose to remain on the property. For our purposes, this case would rate as no-decision. It didn't matter to the judge if the house were haunted or not. The tenants had entered into a legal agreement to lease the property for a certain amount of time. The judge did not accept their argument that the haunting of the residence made it uninhabitable and that the ghostly infestation should void the contract.

There also seemed to be a great deal more than a small amount of collusion in this matter. Justice is not always necessarily fair and there are many types of evil in the world.

THE POLICE FOLLOW A GHOST

Canada claims at least one case of a legally haunted house. We have to search back through the records to 1907 to find it and take a peek into something as mundane as a village constable's daily "occurrence book" to locate where the story begins.

The location of the haunting is in Manitoba and the proceedings that arose from it were held before the King's Bench.

To get an idea of how the haunting began we refer directly to the investigating constable's official log in his "occurrence book."

"Second house east of Marie, on St. John's Avenue, is believed by some people to be haunted at night between 11 and 12 midnight. There are parties of men hanging around this house, also in the basement, awaiting the appearance of the spook. This house is at present unoccupied."

It seemed that a lot of people in the area of Marie and St. John's Avenue were quite interested in ghost hunting. One has to wonder why. Was this ghost really so boisterous? Or maybe it was because this spook had a regular time of appearance, between 11 pm and midnight.

An ambitious newspaper reporter got a peek at the constable's occurrence book and paid a visit to the site of the haunting. Following is the report he filed with his newspaper.

"A North End ghost: There is a ghost in the north end of the city that is causing a lot of trouble to the inhabitants. His chief haunt is the vacant house on St. John's Avenue, near Marie. He appears late at night and performs strange antics so that timid people give the place a wide berth. A number of men have lately made a stand against ghosts in general, and at night they rendezvous in the basement and close around the haunted house to await his ghostship, but so far he still remains at large."

It would have been interesting to hear more about the strange antics but the reporter didn't expand on those. Mostly he just repeated what was written in the police report. The newspaper article was apparently widely read because not only did larger crowds gather outside the haunted house but other reporters showed up and many more stories about the haunting were published.

The owner of the haunted property didn't like this. He was having enough difficulty trying to rent out the vacant house without its having the reputation for being haunted. Now how was he ever going to rent it!!

The owner's only recourse now was to sue the newspaper that had printed the initial story about the haunting, charging damages due to decreased value of the property.

The judge did not agree with the legal theory involved. He noted that it would be practically impossible to pinpoint any specific damages caused by the newspaper named in the suit because the story about the haunted house appeared in more than one newspaper. Additionally, if more than one newspaper were sued it would be impossible to allot the amount of damages to be levied in any equitable fashion. Thus, the judge ruled against the complainant.

However, the property owner appealed to the Manitoba Court of Appeals. The appellate court thought differently on the matter than the lower court. It noted that the original story of the haunting precipitated the later stories and that without this initial impetus the reputation of the house might not have been so severely damaged. The court ruled that a haunted house was by its very nature worth less than a non-haunted house, and that this house was indeed besieged by a specter.

The Manitoba Court of Appeals held the newspaper that printed the initial story about the haunting liable for damages to the property owner in the amount of $1,200 in Canadian currency. It isn't divulged how that amount was determined.

A MODERN LEGALLY HAUNTED HOUSE

All of the other haunted house stories have been leading up to this one. It is a relatively modern story and it deals DIRECTLY with the matter of a legally haunted house. In this case from 1991 the new owner of a home in Nyack, New York found to his dismay that the home he'd just purchased for a great deal of money was haunted - and not by a friendly ghost. He wanted his money returned and the sale voided.

Anyone who has ever purchased a home knows the formidable problem that the unhappy homeowner faced. Once a sale is complete - all the papers had been signed, the deeds registered, the document stamps paid for, the commissions doled out, and the escrows for taxes and insurance filed - it is murderously difficult if not impossible to have these all voided and/or reversed. Once the sale of a home is final THAT IS THAT! You own it and all the hidden problems that might have come with it.

But what if the problem is a ghost? Not just a ghost, but a noisy, destructive and terrifying ghost? What do you do then!! (Information for this story is taken from direct interviews by the author with all of the primary participants).

Jeffrey Stambovsky purchased a Victorian mansion in Nyack, New York from Helen V. Ackley for $650,000. He and his family had been residents of New York City and were seeking the quiet atmosphere in the countryside in Nyack. They instead found themselves imprisoned in a haunted house, stranded far away from everyone they knew who could help and comfort them. Mr. Stambovsky decided that his only recourse was to sue to have the sale of the house vacated: STAMBOVSKY V. ACKLEY.

Real names are used because the proceedings are public record, having been part of a court proceeding. Additional information about this story was obtained through personal interviews with a number of the primary participants - the homeowner and the real estate agent who sold him the house, among them - which gives us a much fuller view of the event.

The official records of this case do not show the type and the scope of the haunting and the effect that it had on the new owners, who were also new parents at the time. The specter that stalked this house was not simply noisy, and not simply mournful. It was loud, it was angry and it seemed intent on driving out the new owners. Household items were broken, everyday objects were misplaced to cause frustration to the owners, and, a shady, frightening figure delighted in terrifying the young one occupying the nursery.

The other party's viewpoint in this matter bears noting. While the existence of the ghost was admitted, it was claimed that the spirit itself was not particularly threatening or violent. The severity of the haunting could be traced primarily to the active imagination and over-sensitivity of the new owners, said the old owner.

Thus, there are two sides seeing the problem very differently. The main point, however, is whether or not the house was haunted and whether the new owners were warned about this beforehand?

The matter reached the Appellate Division of the New York Supreme Court on July 18, 1991. After all of the particulars had been presented before the justices - who were hearing this on appeal - the presiding judge, Justice Rubin, issued his statement.

Justice Rubin: "The usual facts of this case, as disclosed by the record, clearly warrant a grant of equitable relief to the buyer who, as a resident of New York City, cannot be expected to have any familiarity with the folklore of the village of Nyack. Not being a "local" plaintiff could not readily learn that the home he had contracted to purchase is haunted. Whether the source of the spectral apparitions seen by the defendant seller are parapsychic or psychogenic, having reported their presence in both a national publication ("Readers' Digest") and the local press (in 1977 and 1982, respectively) defendant is stopped to deny their existence and, as a matter of law, the house is haunted.

...AS A MATTER OF LAW, THE HOUSE IS HAUNTED... The exact words of an appellate level judge on the New York Supreme Court.

Justice Rubin continued. "...in 1989, the house was included in a five-home walking tour of Nyack and described in a November 27th newspaper article as a "river front Victorian (with ghost)." ...a fair reading of the merger clause reveals that it expressly disclaims only representations made with respect to the physical conditions of the premises and merely makes general reference to representations concerning "any other matter or things affecting or relating to the aforesaid premises." As broad as this language may be, a reasonable interpretation is that its effect is limited to tangible or physical matters and does not extend to paranormal phenomena. Finally, if the language of the contract is to be construed as broadly as defendant urges to encompass the presence of the poltergeists in the house, it cannot be said that she delivered the premises "vacant" in accordance with her obligation under the provisions of the contract rider. In the case at bar, defendant seller deliberately fostered the belief that her home was possessed. Having undertaken to inform the public at large, to whom she has no legal relationship, about the supernatural occurrences on her property, she may be said to owe no less...to her contract vendee".

In other words: Ms. Ackley should've told the Stambovsky's that the house was haunted. She'd told just about everyone else, why not them? Could it be she was afraid that they might not want to buy a haunted house?

Shouldn't the Stambovsky's have found out about the haunting for themselves? After all, it was written up in the Readers' Digest, and had been featured on a walking tour as a haunted house. Not according to the justices.

"Haunting of home is not a condition which can and should be ascertained upon reasonable inspection of the premises by the purchaser. Equity would permit purchaser to rescind contract for sale of home and recover his down payment upon discovery of the home's reputation as being haunted."

And the final legal judgment, which is not as clearly stated as the other remarks follows: Judgement, Supreme Court, New York County (Edward H. Lehner, J.) Entered April 9, 1990, modified on the law and the facts and in exercise of discretion, and the first cause of action seeking rescission of the contract reinstated, without costs.

All of which means: the house has been declared legally haunted, the contract of sale has been voided, and the down payment money has been ordered returned to the purchasers. The scope of this decision almost takes a person's breath away. The justices were very clear and very decisive about their ruling. The house was haunted and the seller had the responsibility to make the buyers aware of this fact because it wasn't something that the purchasers should have been expected to find out on their own.

DIFFERENT TYPES OF GHOSTS

Considering the subject of the different species of ghosts: does there seem a definite difference between the types of ghosts which haunt houses and those which come back to either accuse their murderers or to clear up legal problems and wills?

One of the reasons proving the existence of ghosts has been so difficult is because there are different types - species if you will - of phantasms. Ghosts who have returned to accuse their murderers or to set right matters of inheritance are generally more consciously directed and have a verifiable presence. They can be seen and often heard. And once their mission is completed, they depart.

Note the type of ghosts which haunt houses. They throw things, cause noises and can be either general nuisances or terrifying specters. This type of behavior is usually associated with poltergeists, but for this discussion both types of entities are considered the same species of spirit. In the haunted houses, the troubled spirits seem to be bound to the home and not to any one individual or individuals. Poltergeists are often associated with and created by the psyche of a specific living person.

The other types of ghosts are those which return to set right a wrong. They are more substantive of nature - they have a purpose - and once this mission has been completed, they vanish. These are the types that come back to accuse their murderers and obtain justice.

Earlier it was noted how extremely rare it is for more than one person to see the same ghost at exactly the same time. It is even more exceptionally rare for this to take place in a court of law. The next case involves just that type of sighting and what makes it more unusual is that no one knew about the double sighting until well after the fact.

The extraordinary event is the culmination of a case shadowed with supernatural overtones from the inception. The specifics of the case were reported in a work called "The History of Durham," and the information in the history of Durham book was taken from the local police and court records.

ANNE WALKER'S GHOST

The trial took place in England in 1630 and concerned the murder of young Anne Walker. Anne lived with her cousin and lover John Walker in the village of Great Lumley where there was much gossip about their relationship. Not only did Anne do the housework for her cousin but she also performed more intimate tasks, resulting in her becoming pregnant by him.

To quiet the scandalmongers John Walker dispatched his cousin to be cared for by a woman named Dame Carr in the nearby town of Chester-le-Street. Dame Carr was known for taking in young girls in distress and she was reputed to be a warm and caring person. Several days after Anne had been sent to Dame Carr's a friend of John Walker's named Mark Sharp - a collier (coal-miner) by trade - mysteriously appeared on the doorstep of the home for distressed ladies where the young girl was sent. Sharp told Mrs. Carr that he'd come to take Anne home because her cousin John had had a change of heart and wanted to take care of the girl at home where she rightfully belonged.

Dame Carr was suspicious, but she had to tell Anne the news. Anne was delighted. She hurriedly packed her belongings and rushed out to join Mark Sharp who was waiting for her in his coach. Anne walker was driven away and was never seen alive again.

At this point the story takes a strange turn. A couple of weeks after Anne's murder, her ghost makes an appearance. The site is a grinding mill. It is a very dark night and just coming upon the witching hour. The owner of the mill - James Graime - was still at work, alone and very tired. He was just about to pour a bucketful of fresh corn into the hopper when he was startled by the ghost of Anne Walker. What follows is a description of what happened transcribed from Mr. Graime's account.

"The mill door being shut, there stood a woman in the midst of the floor, with her hair hanging all bloody, with five large wounds on her head." He being much amazed began to bless himself, and at last asked her who she was and what she wanted. She answered, "I am the spirit of Anne Walker, who lived with John Walker. He promised to send me where I should be well looked to and then I should come again and keep his house. I was one night sent away with Mark Sharp, who, upon a certain moor slew me with a pick such as men dig coal with and gave me these five wounds, and after threw my body into a coal pit hard by, and hid the pick under a bank, and his shoes and stockings being bloody he endeavored to wash them, but seeing the blood would not part he hid them there."

The ghost instructed Mr. Graime to tell the authorities about her murder. Why she didn't tell the authorities herself isn't clear. It seems that ghosts in general do not contact the authorities and seem to have a strong aversion for doing so. This is difficult to account for, but does seem to be a fact.

In matters such as this ghosts typically contact close friends or loved ones. Maybe this is because they are the only people that the ghosts trust. And maybe it's because the ghosts are psychically drawn to these people.

However, there isn't any evidence in this case that Anne Walker had ever met Mr. Graime before her death which makes her manifestation to him all the more confounding. Why contact a total stranger!

It's possible that Anne's psychic self was still in a state of shock following her sudden and brutal murder and her spirit "happened upon" the first living human she came across. Or maybe there is some occult law of attachment that caused Anne to be naturally drawn to Mr. Graime's psyche. There isn't any definite answer as to why the ghost of Anne Walker contacted this specific person rather than another.

It certainly wasn't for quick results, however! Mr. Graime did not respond in any way to the ghost's initial visit. He didn't inform the authorities. He didn't go to the murder scene. He did nothing.

This forced a second visit from the ghost. And this time the ghost was angry and in a foul mood. Once again Anne's spirit demanded that something be done about solving her murder and once again Mr. Graime did nothing. Why he still failed to act is unclear. Maybe he thought the sightings of Anne's ghost were hallucinations or maybe he feared that if he told the authorities about the girl's slaying he would be considered the prime suspect.

At any rate, Anne's ghost made a third appearance this time while Mr. Graime was working alone peacefully in his garden. Anne appeared in a terrifying aspect. The furious ghost screeched and flailed, threatening Graime with continuing visitations in ever worsening temper until he did as asked.

Mr. Graime finally went to the authorities and on December 21st he made his deposition with the magistrate. A due search was made for the body of Anne Walker which was located at the bottom of a coal pit on the moor spoken of by the ghost previously. The corpse had five large wounds in its head and the murder weapon along with the bloodstained shoes of the killer were found hard nearby, in the spirit's language. Anne's body was buried so deeply in the coal pit it would not likely have been stumbled upon by a passerby, so how else would Mr. Graime have known where to look for it if not by the direction of the ghost?

Some claimed that he knew where it was because he was the murderer. However, Anne was last seen alive departing with Mark Sharp and this was testimony given in court by Dame Carr. In addition to this, it was Sharp's bloody shoes that were found with the dead girl's body as well as - later - his pick used in his collier work. Mister Graime would've had no known reason to kill Anne Walker. There wasn't any evidence to show that he'd ever met the woman.

At any rate, there was enough evidence to arrest John Walker and Mark Sharp for the murder of Anne Walker. But this did not put an end to the paranormal activities concerning this case. In fact, they became even more potent and unique.

During the actual trial, an apparition was independently seen in the courtroom by two different people from two different locations in the room. One of the witnesses of the ghost was Mr. Fairbair, the jury foreman. The other witness was none other than the presiding judge who at the time of his sighting was so overwhelmed by it that he adjourned proceedings for the day.

Both men saw the same apparition at the same time and it wasn't the ghost of Anne Walker. It was a different ghost. Both men viewed the apparition of a baby. The ghostly figure floated above the shoulder of defendant Mark Sharp as if to accuse him of the murder.

Why a baby? Anne Walker was well-along in her pregnancy when she was murdered. Presumably the ghost that was seen by the judge and the foreman was that of Anne's murdered unborn child. Neither the judge nor the foreman made their sightings known until after the trial was concluded; and neither knew what the other had seen until much later.

Shortly after the trial, the foreman made a sworn statement, describing the apparition he'd seen in court. And the judge? He also revealed his sighting soon after the trial, when his memory was still clear. In a letter to a friend - Mr. Serjeant Hutton - the judge wrote of the apparition he'd seen in court, describing it and noting the chilling affect it had had upon him.

In addition to these two sightings, official records of the trial of Mark Sharp and John Walker speak of an unusual "spooky" atmosphere that lingered over the proceedings. The sense of the supernatural was strong! Did other people beside the judge and the foreman see apparitions in the courtroom, hear strange sounds? Only the two mentioned are on record for certain, but how many others weren't recorded?

What was the outcome of the trial? Both Mark Sharp and John Walker were convicted of the murder of Anne Walker. Both were executed with the primary evidence having been supplied by a ghost.

A FAULTY SPIRIT

Sometimes a medium has to be especially careful to take note of the spirit with whom she is communicating. One spirit is not just as good as another. Mrs. L.D. McMasters learned this lesson in her trial and the subsequent rehearing: Mrs. L.D. McMasters, Plff. in Err., v. State of Oklahoma. The appellate court hearing was held on June 13, 1922. The presiding judge was Thomas H. Doyle and the associate judge was E.S. Bessey. The names of the judge are an interesting coincidence which will be noted later by the judges themselves. The case is a simple one on the surface about a person - Mrs. McMasters - who was arrested for telling fortunes, which was a very popular business in the 1920's. Bessie Jones was a young woman who was working undercover for the Oklahoma City Police Department and who went to the home of Mrs. McMasters to have a "reading" done for her.

Mrs. McMasters ushered her patron into the spirit room, requested from Bessie what it was she was seeking an answer for, and then dropped into a trance. While in this state, the supposed-medium contacted the spirit of Minnehaha. Minnehaha revealed to Mrs. McMasters that her client would soon have a better job offer, go on a long trip, then marry a wealthy man after having to decide between two young and virile men vying for her attentions.

It certainly sounds like a future that any young woman of that era would dream of. Mrs. McMasters was probably shocked because, after giving this good news - and receiving a payment of $1.00 for her services - she was promptly arrested by the undercover policewoman. Mrs. McMasters was taken to court, put on trial for fortune telling for hire, and was duly convicted - which

106

she should have foreseen if she could read the future. Right? She was given a sentence of thirty days in jail and fined $50.00.

Mrs. McMasters appealed the ruling, claiming that her religious freedom was being impinged upon. After all, she was a spiritualist who was merely contacting a spirit on the other side for the purpose of advising a client. Since her patron seemed to be a lovelorn young lady, Minnehaha seemed the most logical to ask for assistance on matters of the heart.

While the facts of the case are clear and speak for themselves - Mrs. McMasters was illegally practicing fortune telling for hire from her home and not from a duly authorized spiritualist church - the detailed remarks that it drew from the appellate level justices are quite noteworthy, along with the fair amount of humor interjected.

In this case not only is it best to let the evidence speak for itself, but to allow the justices to do so as well. Thus, they are quoted extensively through Justice E.S. Bessey who rendered the court's opinion.

Justice Bessey: "There have been and now are many persons of extraordinary high mentality and intelligence who implicitly believe that communication can be had with departed spirits through a spiritualist medium. One of the most prominent adherents of this faith A. Conan Doyle (who should not be confused with Thomas H. Doyle, presiding judge of this court), claims that departed souls are enveloped with a kind of external body, capable of being photographed, and that such photographs are inexistence; also that he has a physical writing of a letter by spirit friend..."

At this point the judge makes a most vital observation. This has to do with the nature of the spirit of Minnehaha, an oversight made by the medium which is astonishing in its obviousness.

The judge goes on: "The legendary Minnehaha never existed in the flesh; hence a continuity of her spirit cannot exist in the spirit world. Unlike Conan Doyle, this medium produced no photograph of the spirit of Minnehaha. Her identity was not established. Some unknown playful spirit may have deceived the medium, or she may have intended to deceive her client, Bessie.

The judge revealed that he was quite astute in matters of the spirit world. He notes that a continuity of existence is to be inferred if there are to be spirits on the other side to contact. They must first have had an earthly existence. He also showed an awareness that other spirits may appear to use a false identity when communicating with a medium so that the medium can herself be tricked.

This judge was also aware of Conan Doyle's extensive research into the paranormal and that he gave credence to both the spirit photographs and spirit writing that the author claimed to possess. In regard to the current matter at hand, the judge believed that Mrs. McMasters most likely had consciously used the so-called spirit of Minnehaha because Minnehaha would've been the best suited for her love lost client.

Did Mrs. McMasters realize that Minnehaha was a purely fictional character that had never existed in reality? Unfortunately, this is not made known at any point. What if Minnehaha had been a historical figure? The outcome may have been different. This is what Justice Doyle had to say: "If sure of her identity, it would be well worth a dollar of any girl's money to have the benefit of the advice of the sparkling, romantic spirit of Minnehaha.

Justice E. S. Bessey then added his comments, also noting an unusual similarity of names that had come up in this case, comparing his name to that of Mrs. McMasters's patron whose first name was Bessie. Justice Bessey: "While A. Conan Doyle should not be confused with "Thomas H. Doyle" (the other judge) neither should Bessie, the medium's patron, be confused with E. S. Bessey, associate judge of this court and writer of this opinion. I am reliably informed that there is no relationship either by affinity or consanguity, between either of the Doyles or either of the Besseys.

Justice Bessey next discusses applicable laws concerning trade regulation and how they relate to mediums. Justice Bessey:

"Verily, the spirit of regulation is abroad in the land. For some time most of the states have been regulating the mediums of communication between human beings such as telephone and telegraph. How this state proposes to regulate the mediums communication with the spirit world ...can the state constitutionally prohibit communication with the spirit world, with which, so far as I am advised, we are at peace. If it cannot, can it, under the Fourteenth Amendment, deny the mediums of such communication a reasonable compensation

for the services rendered? These queries appear to be pertinent in the instant case. However, assuming that the state in question is not in contravention of the commerce clause of the Federal Constitution, and that the state has the power to regulate, I concur, because the medium in question never filed her schedule of rates with the state corporation commission."

Who Justice Bessey is concurring with is the presiding judge, Doyle, who affirmed the lower court's finding that Mrs. McMasters was guilty and subject to the verdict rendered. At face value - prima facie - what Judge Bessey just said was that Mrs. McMasters was guilty because she failed to register her rates for her services with the proper state authority, not that she was guilty of fraud or racketeering.

However, a closer look at the applicable law shows that

110

even if she had done so she would have been in violation of the regulation, as follows: IT SHALL BE UNLAWFUL FOR ANY PERSON OR PERSONS, PRETENDING OR PROFESSING TO TELL FORTUNES BY THE USE OF ANY SUBTLE CRAFT, MEANS OR DEVICE WHATSOEVER, EITHER BY PALMISTRY, CLAIRVOYANCY, OR OTHERWISE, PLYING HIS OR HER TRADE, ART OR PROFESSION WITHIN THE STATE OF OKLAHOMA, TO MAKE ANY CHARGE THEREFORE EITHER DIRECTLY OR INDIRECTLY OR TO RECEIVE ANY GIFT, DONATION OR SUBSCRIPTION BY ANY MEANS WHATSOEVER FOR THE SAME.

You can't be much clearer than that - no fortune telling except for fun and games and without even the hint of pay. The Fourteenth Amendment (prohibiting slavery, or work without remuneration of some type) does not apply here.

Mrs. McMasters appealed the original ruling, claiming that her right to freely practice the religion of her choice was being violated. She argued that she was a practicing spiritualist and among the major beliefs of spiritualism is the ability to contact spirits on the other side. However, this is what the law says on that matter: LAWS ARE MADE FOR THE GOVERNMENT OF ACTIONS, AND, WHILE THEY CANNOT INTERFERE WITH MERE RELIGIOUS BELIEFS, THEY MAY WITH

PRACTICES.... THEY MAY WITH PRACTICES. This is why such matters as polygamy and various beliefs that deny medical treatment to people who need it are not allowed by the legal system. These are practices which the state can regulate.

The three justices who heard the appeal all agreed: Mrs. McMasters was guilty and the verdict was affirmed. Justice Bessey suggested that, while neither he nor the others could alter the sentencing, that the jail time be dropped from the penalty for Mrs. McMasters.

This case was vitally important for many reasons. One of which is that IT SET A PRECEDENT, making it unlawful to claim a fictitious being as a person who can be contacted beyond the grave since this fictitious character did not possess continuity of existence. Prior to making their decision, the justices sought legal precedents but did not find any. Therefore, their opinions would mark a precedent. This is most likely why each had a great deal to add to the findings of the court, although it was Justice Bessey who formally gave the opinion on record.

The question remains: What if, instead of Minnehaha, Mrs. McMaster had contacted a deceased friend or relative of her patron, and what if she had filed her rates with the state commerce commission? What would have been the court's findings then since the justice's primary concern was that Mrs. McMasters had contacted a non-existent being (whatever that may be?) and that she had not properly filed her rates.

ANOTHER SPIRIT FINANCIAL ADVISOR

No matter WHY financial advice is given from beyond the grave, it is a fact of reality that spirits have provided it. This can be verified as a fact through various court records. One of the first examples is from a matter heard in 1901 in Dean v. Ross which was a very common type of proceeding from the times.

Mrs. Ross was a medium and Mrs. Dean was her client. Mrs. Ross had been holding regular "sittings" with the elderly widow in order to contact Mrs. Dean's departed husband. During one of these "sittings" the spirit of Mrs. Dean's husband allegedly advised her to transfer 15 security bonds worth a great deal of money into the medium's name. It seems pretty obvious that what this medium was seeing was her OWN future - in retirement.

Nonetheless, Mrs. Dean did as instructed and transferred the bonds. It isn't recorded why her husband's spirit might have wanted her to transfer the bonds to the medium or how it was supposed to benefit his widow.

However, after the passage of time and the commencement of a new marriage, the former Mrs. Dean got suspicious and sued the medium for return of the bonds. The subject matter of the case was relatively common because this type of swindle was being played on vulnerable elderly moneyed widows across the country by unscrupulous con-artists. These were the types of cheats that the great Harry Houdini was waging war against - quite successfully.

What made Dean v. Ross so remarkable was the commentary of the presiding judge. The following are his instructions to the jury: If there was a message received from the husband, and the defendant simply delivered the message, believing it to be true, to this plaintiff, why then that would not be any false statement with the reference to the transaction; that would be a true statement, and I meant you to understand that then the plaintiff could not recover, if that was a fact and that was a real communication.

The judge is allowing the jury to determine whether it believed that the communication between the medium and the spirit of the dead husband had or had not actually occurred. If it had and the medium honestly believed that the message had really come from the late Mr. Dean then the instructions from the spirit to his wife to transfer the security bonds to the medium was proper and valid. The judge was ruling that the ghost of the late Mr. Dean could - both legally and actively - still give instructions on how his earthly possessions were to be distributed.

However, in this trial the jury believed that the accused had acted in a fraudulent manner and held that the transfer of bonds had been enacted illegally. This does not mean that the jury vetoed the existence of ghosts, just that in this one case the medium was a crook and probably made up the entire supposed conversation with the late Mr. Dean.

A GAELIC SPEAKING GHOST

The next case involves two witnesses to the same ghost but from greatly different vantage points. Again, it is an extremely rare occurrence and one of the very few times ghostly evidence was given in court by TWO different people which is all the more powerful.

The events that led to the trial took place in the mid-18th century just after Prince Charlie had been defeated in his attempt to secure the liberty of Scotland. A garrison had been left behind in the Highlands until the situation was stabilized. It was under these conditions that in 1740 one of the English soldiers belonging to this garrison mysteriously disappeared.

The 1740's was a time when English soldiers were quite unpopular on Scottish soil. It wasn't a very good decision made by Sergeant Arthur Davies of General Guise's Regiment of Foot to go off on his own to hunt some grouse on that fateful day in 1745 when he disappeared. It was even less advisable to wear his valuable gold rings and carry a bag of gold pieces.

Why take a bag of gold with you to go grouse hunting? Maybe the sergeant didn't trust his fellow soldiers at the barracks, or maybe he was afraid that the people of the nearby village would break in and steal his money while away. Either way, he lost both his life and his bag of gold that day.

It was only through the intercession of the dead man's ghost that the murder was brought to light five years later. Five years later! Note the continued consistency of the time lag between a person's death and his spirit's own realization of it. Why else would it take five years for the ghost to appear if not because it took that long for the spirit to realize what had happened?

To whom did the ghost appear? Attired in his blue uniform, the ghost of Arthur Davies appeared to a Scotsman named Alexander MacPherson as the man stood alone in the field near the site of Davies' murder. They were complete strangers to each other.

Note this second consistency of ghostly behavior - the person to whom the spirit appeared. Not to the authorities of the town, not to an official in the British armed forces, but to a total stranger. A Gaelic-speaking Scotsman no less! The fact that he spoke Gaelic is important and the reason it's important will be noted later.

When the ghost appeared to Mr. MacPherson, he simply said, "I am Sergeant Davies," after which he motioned for the startled Scotsman to follow him. MacPherson went after him a short distance across the field to where the apparition stopped and pointed, saying to the effect, "My bones lie there. Bury them as a good Christian would." Then the spirit vanished.

As in the story with Anne Walker, MacPherson did not do as the ghost had requested. He turned and went home. However, on the next day, MacPherson returned to the spot that the spirit had pointed out to him and found the body of Davies partially buried in a peat bog. MacPherson hauled the remains the rest of the way out of the slimy bog but did no more. He left the body to lie where it was and returned home without telling anyone about it.

Again like the Anne Walker story, the angry ghost made yet another appearance and in a terrifying form to MacPherson. Naked and horrific from decay, the specter confronted MacPherson in a barn where he and other farmhands were living. The furious spirit demanded a proper burial for its body.

People who deny the existence of ghosts and base this on the lack of simultaneous sightings are thwarted by this case. And doubly so! Not only did TWO people later see the ghost of Davies at the same time, but they saw him from different angles.

Here the story becomes unique. Isabel MacHardie also saw the ghost but from another location in the barn. She saw MacPherson and the spirit from behind and was shocked by the ghost's gruesome appearance. In court she stated under oath that she saw, "Something naked come in at the door and go straight to MacPherson's bed."

The woman was so terrified that she leapt into her own bed and yanked the covers over her head. Isabel MacHardie didn't hear what the ghost said to MacPherson. One thing that is known is that MacPherson sought the identities of the murderers. The ghost told him, "Duncan Terig and Alex MacDonald."   MacPherson took this evidence to the authorities and Terig and MacDonald were arrested for the murder of Arthur Davies.

Just on the word of that one man?   No. There was additional incriminating evidence. About five years earlier the two suspects had suddenly come up with enough money to buy and stock a farm. A bagful of gold would be just about the right amount to pay for such a purchase. That's what Arthur Davies was carrying with him when he was murdered.

Mr. MacPherson gave his testimony in court, remarking that the ghost had spoken to him in, "As good Gaelic as he had ever heard in Lochaber." The defense attorney pounced on this statement, crying out, "Pretty well, for the ghost of an English sergeant."

Arthur Davies was an Englishman and his ghost would be expected to speak in the King's English rather than Highlands Gaelic. This was part of the reason that Terig and MacDonald were acquitted. Prejudice was probably the major reason. Why would a jury of Scotsman convict two of their own for murdering an English soldier stationed on their soil after the quelling of an insurrection in which Scotsman were killing Englishmen without penalty?

Anyway - the ghost got what he wanted - a decent burial at last.

THE FIRST PHOTOGRAPHERS OF GHOSTS

Spirit photography - or the act of taking photographs of spirits on the other plane - had its beginning almost with the inception of the photographic process itself. It's a fascinating branch of the spiritualist movement in that it came about accidentally and, even though some people practice this form of astral communication to this day, its real popularity lasted only a few years. As we all know, "doctored" photographs can now be made to be so authentic looking that by that very fact the use of spirit photography can no longer ever be used as evidence. But for a brief time in the 1800's it could.

One of the earliest accounts of a spirit appearing on a picture was recorded in October of 1862. The photograph was taken in Boston, Massachusetts in a studio operated by a man named Mumler, a person who until then had been a simple practitioner of the new technology of photography. He did not plan or set out to take a picture of a ghost.

One of Mr. Mumler's patrons - Mr. Gardner - had sat for a photograph in Mumler's studio and when he studied the finished product he noted to his astonishment that also displayed on the photograph was the form of a cousin of his who had died twelve years before. When he sat for the picture Mr. Gardner had been alone: no one else in the scene. Not until after the exposure did his cousin appear on the picture.

This event radically changed the life and the business of Mr. Mumler. News of the spirit photograph was widely and rapidly spread. Soon spiritualists from all over the world were swarming to his small studio in Boston to see who would develop on their photographs, beside themselves (literally and figuratively). Few left disappointed. Mumler produced a great many spirit photographs to the satisfaction of his patrons

Early in 1863, however, Mumler's first client - Mr. Gardner - discovered by some means that at least two of the Mumler spirit photographs were fakes. Nonetheless, Gardner and the majority of Mumler's patrons still accepted the authenticity of many of the photographs, arguing that the spirit faces that appeared in their particular photographs were undoubtedly of those of departed friends or relatives - UNDOUBTEDLY!

In addition to this, Mumler's photographic techniques had been observed and tested by experts who could not detect any fraud involved. It is common practice in the field of paranormal investigation to treat each case on its own merits, meaning that while some cases indicated fraud, other cases seemed genuine and, this being true, Mumler was not branded as a charlatan or fraud. However, after the accusations, his business declined. It declined so much that he closed his studio in Boston and moved to New York City.

In New York City he continued taking spirit photographs but here too he was soon brought under suspicion of fraudulent behavior. Here he was taken to court. However, the only evidence brought forward against him was of the hearsay variety. In fact, according to the court's findings there were not any grounds for Mumler's arrest other than discrimination, specifically based on one government official's strong disbelief in spiritualism.

Not only was there not any substantial evidence presented against Mumler, there was a great deal of testimony in support of him from patrons who swore under oath that the spirit photographs were genuine. The judge summarily dismissed the charges and took the district attorney to task for bringing such a flimsy case before him.

During the last three years of the 19th century spirit photography was all the rage, as the saying goes. Some of the photographers were genuine believers, some were frauds, and some were a mixture of both. A Frenchman named Buguet (pictured below) falls into this third class. His is a very interesting and confusing story.

In 1874 Buguet opened a photographic studio in London for the express purpose of producing spirit photographs. By all accounts his work was far superior to the others of his day. Instead of blotchy, fuzzy, ill-defined photographs his were clear, professional and graced with easily recognized spirit faces. Could this be because he was better at manufacturing - in a fraudulent way - supposed spirit photos than anyone else, not that he was such an accomplished artist?

Many of Buguet's photographs were of famous people, including: Allan Kardec, Charles Dickens, and Stainton Moses. Well - famous in their day. Most people know who Dickens is, but what about Allan Kardec and Stainton Moses? Allan Kardec was the father of spiritism which is different from spiritualism because it accepts the concept of reincarnation. Stainton Moses was a very prominent spiritualist in his day. He wrote what many considered the bible of spiritualism, a brilliant work called "Spirit Teachings."

Mr. Moses was later to swear under oath that at the time Buguet was photographing him in his studio, he was directing his thoughts directly to Buguet's studio. No, a person does not have to be deceased to be able to perform astral projection which is what Mr. Moses was alluding to.

Stainton Moses's telepathic delivery of his features to Buguet for the purposes of showing up on a photographic plate was not the first such instance in which Mr. Moses performed such a feat. He also "sat" telepathically for a drawing made of him by the clairvoyant artist Frank Leah, a famous portrait artist of the day.

Buguet, however, was not a true disciple of the movement

it seems. He was arrested for fraud in June of 1875 and put on trial by the French government. Not only did he refuse to present a defense, he plead guilty to all charges. And this was despite all of the testimonials by satisfied clients who refused to believe that the spirit photographs he'd taken were not genuine.

Buguet admitted to the court that most of the photographs were achieved by means of double exposure and through the use of paid assistants dressing up as spirits and sitting in the background while the photo was being taken. Artificial heads and a closet full of costume clothing was later found on the premises of Buguet's studio to verify his confession.

It is an extreme irony that despite his admission of guilt witness after witness came to the stand to profess belief in him and his photographic process. The faces in the photos belonged to their friends and relatives!!! They swore to it and nothing would change their opinion. After all wouldn't the patrons be the best judges on the physical appearance of their friends and relatives?

What is to follow is a brief excerpt of actual courtroom testimony - verbatim - taken of the judge questioning one of the witnesses and then questioning Buguet.

Witness: "The portrait of my wife which I had specifically asked for is so like her that when I showed it to one of my relatives he exclaimed, 'It's my cousin!'"

The judge then addressed the defendant: "Was that chance, Buguet?"

Buguet: "Yes, pure chance. I had no photograph of Mademoiselle Dessenon."

The witness refused to believe Buquet, saying: "My children, like myself, thought the likeness perfect. When I showed them the picture they cried, 'It's mamma!' A very fortunate chance! I am convinced it is my wife."

The judge then addresses the witness, motioning to the physical evidence that was brought in to prove Buguet's fraudulent activities. Judge: "You see this doll and the rest of these things?"

Witness: "There is nothing there in the least like the photograph which I obtained."

None of the fabricated heads and dolls were anything like the face or form of the witness's wife. The witness was steadfast in his belief in the spirit photograph. So too were the many who followed him to the stand and were asked basically the same questions.

How to account for such a situation? Stainton Moses and other prominent spiritualists of the day accused the French clergy of waging a vendetta against spiritualism. The government was the clergy's ally, they argued, and accused by them to have produced the false evidence against Buguet and "planted" it in his studio. Maybe so - but what of Buguet?

He confessed to faking the photographs and would not defend himself in the least. This in itself is quite suspicious. Most likely he was either bribed to confess his guilt or was coerced by government officials to do so.

Why? Why would the government so fear this man? Maybe the charges by Stainton Moses and the other spiritualists were true: it was a good old fashioned witch hunt. And in that vein, we will move to the next chapter but remain in France to investigate one of the most historic trials for witchcraft ever held - Cideville.

FRENCH WIZARD AND HIS GHOSTS

Most people have heard of Salem and of some of the more gruesome witch trials in England. Very few have heard about the trial in Cideville, France. Oddly enough, of all the trials for witchcraft ever held, this may have been the only one in which the accused was a genuine witch.

By witch I mean the old-fashioned term for a witch. An evil person who is in league with the Devil and has acquired and used satanic powers to harm his fellow man and to acquire money and goods for him or herself. I do not mean the modern day witch

126

- a rather benign, benevolent person who uses good magic to help his fellow man and better him or herself. The type of witch to be examined now uses demonic familiars to help in his evil work, causes specters, poltergeists and wicked ghosts to appear for the purpose of terrifying people and who spreads pandemonium in general. It is the ability to raise ghosts which qualifies the witch in this section to be included in the book.

This is a very complex and convoluted case but the "devil is in the details" as the saying goes (it fits this so well). An aged shepherd who was known as a wizard lived near the town of Yvetot in France. This wizard had several "pupils" who were out in the world working magic, not quite like Harry Potter.

A peasant who lived nearby was suffering from an illness and was being treated by the wizard. In March of 1849 the priest of the nearest large city, Cideville, visited the ailing man. The priest's name was Tinel. During his visit, Tinel suggested that the ailing man consult a legitimate physician instead of the wizard. Tinel was unaware that the wizard was hiding out of sight in the next room while this advice was being given. The wizard was not happy.

The wizard was made even more miserable a few days later when he was arrested for practicing medicine without a license. He was incarcerated for several months and understandably thought that the person responsible for his arrest had been Tinel, the priest of Cideville. The wizard swore that he would have revenge on Tinel.

Living in the area was a dull-witted shepherd named Thorel. He claimed to be one of the wizard's "pupils" and boasted of having many powers. Thorel was to be the instrument of the wizard's revenge on Tinel.

The priest of Cideville also was employed as - what would be called today - a tutor, and had several students of a more legitimate nature. A group of the priest's students attended a public sale of wood on November 25, 1850 in Cideville. Thorel - the wizard's accomplice - also attended this public sale of wood. While at the sale, Thorel touched two of Tinel's pupils. By touching them he theoretically made the students vulnerable to the spells of the still nameless wizard.

The students were fifteen-year-old Lemonier and twelve-year-old Bunel. Now THEY were to be the direct instruments of the wizard's revenge. The two students did their matriculation at the priest's comfortable home. Once they had been touched by Thorel the priest's home became a household thrown into pandemonium.

A quick recap: the wizard WAS imprisoned for practicing medicine without a license, the wizard DID swear vengeance on

128

Tinel, Thorel was a pupil of the wizard's, the priest DID have the two aforementioned pupils studying under him, and after the public wood sale in Cideville the Tinel household was suddenly cast into a paranormal uproar.

The occurrences that took place at the Tinel household were verified by several witnesses while under oath in a court of law. The chief witnesses were Tinel's two students who were tormented by various psychic monstrosities.

The assaults began on the Tinel household the next day after the public sale of wood, November 26, 1850. The initial disturbances were noises like the soft blows of a hammer which started while the students were studying at about 5 p.m. The pounding became louder when Tinel said, "Plus fort."

Whatever was doing the hammering began to rap out popular tunes of the day, then tables moved across the room by themselves, and next various household items became threatening projectiles flying about the house. Fifteen-year-old Lemonier was beset by a phantom black hand which followed him about and frequently jostled him. In addition to this, a full phantom form also terrorized him. As Lemonier stated in court: "A kind of human phantom, clad in a blouse, haunted me for fifteen days wherever I went; none but myself could see it." He was also unceremoniously dragged by the leg about the house by a mysterious force.

One day, Thorel, the wizard's partner in vengeance, found a reason to visit the Tinel house. The priest allowed him entrance and immediately demanded of Thorel that he apologize to Lemonier for tormenting him. Thorel knelt before the boy and begged his forgiveness all the while violently tugging on the student's clothing.

Thorel had the audacity to return to the priest's house the next day. The mayor was visiting Tinel when Thorel arrived and the city official was a witness to what took place. Thorel stalked Tinel, attempting to touch him and thereby place the curse of the unnamed wizard upon him. Tinel understood this and fended the man off with his cane. The priest escaped Thorel, but Thorel later charged the priest with assault for striking him with the cane! Assault and libel were the two charges leveled by Thorel against Tinel which was the actual cause of the trial. During its course, however, the spectral attack on Tinel's home became a prominent matter.

Concerning some of the pertinent testimony relating to the haunting of the priest's house and his students, Lemonier testified about Thorel's first visit to the premises: "As soon as I saw him I recognized the phantom which had haunted me for a fortnight, and as I said to M. Tinel 'There is the man who follows me.'"

Twelve-year-old Bunel, the other student, corroborated Lemonier's testimony. He told the court that on November 26, 1850 he heard first a rush of wind, then a tapping on the wall. Bunel also heard the musical knocking, saw furniture flying through the air, and verified that Lemonier had told Tinel that Thorel was the exact duplicate of the phantom that had been plaguing him.

The haunting of the priest's home became widely known throughout France. Crowds of sightseers visited the house to see the paranormal phenomena, ranging from the common laborer to nobility.

In the legal proceedings brought against Tinel, Thorel claimed that the priest - a powerful person in Cideville - had defamed him by publicly declaring him to be a warlock. As his defense, Tinel stated that Thorel was a warlock, working through the auspices of the unnamed wizard, and that the proof of it lay in the disturbances that had wracked his home.

Tinel summoned numerous witnesses to give testimony to the phenomena that was raging in his home and to verify its authenticity. Following is a recapitulation of the testimony, given by people from all walks of life, including trained professionals in various fields who supplied expert testimony in their field of expertise.

A land surveyor testified that the raps occurred when he had placed one of the boys in an attitude which he felt made a hoax impossible. A gentleman who "took all possible precautions," was entertained by "a noise which performed the tunes demanded." A Mister Huet touched a table with his finger and received responsive raps which answered questions, "at the very place where I struck, and beneath my finger. I cannot explain the fact, which, I am convinced was not caused by the child, nor by anyone in the house."

A Mister Cheval slept in the boy's room with the pillow flying out from under his head. When he lay down between the children with his feet on theirs and their hands in his, the coverlet of the bed arose and floated away. The Marquis de Mireville was startled by having his raps answered. Madame de St. Victor was jostled and her clothes tugged on when no one was near her.
A Le Seigneur who was a farmer saw many objects rise and fly about. Also, when he was on the road between Cideville and Anzoonville, "I saw stones come to us, without striking us, hurled by some invisible force."

What to make of all this? While many of the effects sound like typical poltergeist activity this case is very different. The activity was caused and directed at the Tinel household by a person of this world who appeared to have had contact with evil forces on

132

the other side who would do his bidding. The only questions is, WHO that person was: Thorel or the unnamed wizard who for some reason was never identified?

The judge de paix in this case made the decision in a roundabout way. By dismissing Thorel's charges against Tinel accusing him of libel by calling him publicly a warlock, the judge decreed that the statement by Tinel was factual: Thorel was a warlock. Unfortunately, this is where the story ends and a final conclusion to this feud is not recorded.

HAUNTED USED CAR LOT

The next case brings us back to relatively modern times - the early 1960's. The year is 1960 to be exact, and the place is a town in California named Lynwood. What happened here on a used car lot is more like a poltergeist infestation rather than a typical ghost haunting, but it is different enough from a common poltergeist experience to span occult genres.

Once again, a poltergeist is primarily an occult entity of one form or another that usually haunts a person while a ghost is a spirit of one form or another which haunts a building or a location, and, on occasion, it enters a person's dreams. Either can possess intelligent design. These are the basic comparisons between the two forces. What happened in Lynwood, California is best termed a haunting of a used car lot by poltergeist-like methods.

The haunting began abruptly at 9:30 a.m. on September 9, 1960 when rocks began showering onto the car lot. The barrage lasted from 9:30 am of that day until 4:30 p.m. of that day and then the first day's assault was over. The lot was left strewn with over two hundred rocks and other assorted objects, many of which had dented several of the cars on the premises. During the cannonade, the projectiles fell at three minute intervals and sailed in a horizontal direction after falling a short distance downward from a clear sky. It was as if they were caught by a fierce wind and then blown into that straight-line path. But there wasn't any wind.

The police were summoned to the lot and a thorough investigation was set underway. About twenty police officers dispersed over the area surrounding the used car lot, looking for a hypothetical culprit who possessed something like a huge catapult. What else could be used for such an attack? That was the authority's best suggestion.

It seemed somewhat appropriate, too, when considering that all of the rocks had fallen within a fifty foot radius and would have to have been ejected from a catapult-like device within a block or two distant from the target.

Neither a suspect nor a catapult were discovered during the

search of the neighborhood and beyond. Even though the bombardment had ceased, the police decided it was a good idea to keep the car lot under surveillance. Police officers were station at elevated locations near the car lot. While one of the officers was peering through binoculars onto the target area he witnessed a man depart the used car lot office, pick up a handy rock, and slam it against the side of one of the cars. That must've been their man!

The policeman on the tower who'd been observing through binoculars contacted his compatriots below by walkie-talkie and told them who to apprehend. They did as they were instructed and the case seemed solved.

The suspect was apprehended on suspicion of vandalism. However, as he was being led away, the bombardment resumed and even the suspect was struck by one of the stones. Nevertheless, he was arrested and taken to jail anyway. The police then assumed he must've had an accomplice. So another search of the area was made and again nothing was discovered.

Matters still looked dim for the suspect. It was discovered that he had been a former employee of the used car lot where he'd been responsible for detailing the vehicles. He resented this menial work and the low wages. The suspect had worked as a detailer at other car washing places as well but there weren't any stone throwing incidences at any of those.

The rain of stones and other projectiles on the Lynwood used car lot ceased as abruptly as it had started. The only suspect was placed on trial. The arresting officer was asked if he had actually seen the defendant throw any of the rocks and he admitted that he hadn't.

The defense attorney pointed out that the cannonade of the used car lot continued even after the suspect had been arrested and was sitting in jail. How then could he possibly be the cause of the vandalism?

It was at this point that the prosecuting attorney stated that the suspect had been arrested for interfering with the investigation rather than being the cause of the disturbance. The defense attorney arose to this and demanded an immediate acquittal.

The judge agreed, dismissing the charge entirely, claiming that there wasn't any genuine evidence against the suspect on any counts. However, his observation of the cause of the attack on the used car lot was highly noteworthy. An assault of stones and other materials had occurred. Of that, there was no doubt. There also wasn't any doubt that no one could be charged with the crime - no one human that is. The judge's official verdict was that the assault on the used car lot was the result of "Cosmic forces." Another word for ghosts?

CHASED INTO HELL BY A DEVIL

This is a very rare case from the English law courts of the late 17th century. But the facts are indisputable and the forces involved can only be described as supernatural.

Like so many of the cases examined in this book the charges in this current pleading are of common libel. But because the matter had been taken before a court of law the details of the events and the findings of proof are recorded in history.

What is to follow is a documented sighting of a man's ghost - BY MANY WITNESSES - at the time of his death. A death which occurred hundreds of miles from where the sighting was made and by three individuals who could not possibly have otherwise known of the man's demise.

On Friday, May 15, 1687, Captains Barnaby, Bristow, and Brown were shooting rabbits on the isle of Stromboli. There were many others in the hunting part, including native bush beaters whose purpose was to drive the prey from under cover. It was about quarter to four in the afternoon when everybody was gathered in the same general location when they all beheld a man in black and a man in gray running toward them.

Captain Barnaby shouted, "The foremost is Old Booty, my next door neighbor."

The two men in the distance continued their sprint across the landscape until they disappeared into the flames of a volcano, reaching upward out of a crevice in the ground. This entire event was noted in the logbooks of the three captains.

Several months passed and the three captains returned to their homeland in England. It was October of that same year and Captain Barnaby - one of those who'd seen Old Booty - was attending a party with his wife. Also at this party was the widow of Old Booty. In a chance remark, Mrs. Barnaby said to her husband the captain, "My dear, Old Booty is dead."

Captain Barnaby lightly replied to this: "We all saw him run into hell." He was referring to the volcano flames that Old Booty had leapt into.

The wife of Old Booty was in hearing distance of this remark. She was incensed by the claim that her dear departed husband had gone down to hell.

Remember, back in 1687 it was commonly believed that hell was under the surface of the earth and that it was truly a place of fire and brimstone. Also, when Captain Barnaby stated that he'd seen Old Booty run into hell he wasn't being quaint or funny; he was being serious. He believed that Old Booty had truly ran into the jaws of hell, or rather, was chased there.

Old Booty's wife did not like that disparagement of her

138

dead husband's character and promptly sued Captain Barnaby for libel. The hearing was convened in the Court of the King's Bench (1687-88) during which the clothing that Old Booty had been wearing at the time of his death in England - not hundreds of miles away on the Isle of Stromboli - was put on display as evidence for the defense. It was singed - as by fire. Hellfire?

The date and the hour of the man's death were recorded in the court documents. Then the defense brought out the three logbooks of the three captains who'd witnessed Old Booty's gallop into hell. Each captain had written a detailed description of the sighting. These were entered as evidence.

The three journals all revealed that the sighting of Old Booty running toward the flames of hell had occurred within two minutes of the time of his actual recorded death in England hundreds of miles away. Within two minutes! How could they have known of Old Booty's death unless what the three men had seen truly was the dead man's rush toward perdition?

The court agreed. There could be no libel granted if the statement made was true. And the Court deemed that it was true: the witnesses on that day in May actually saw Old Booty being chased into hell. The charges were dismissed.

I chose this to be the next-to-last case to examine because it is a perfect blend of the ultra-mundane - taxes - with the supernatural. Two subjects that are rarely dealt with at the same time.

It's about a haunted house in Chicago, Illinois in the year 1912. The story, oddly enough, received wide coverage in the French publication, *Journal des bats*. The account concerns a property assessment being altered due to the hauntedness of a particular building.

The piece of real estate in question was owned by Mr. J. Denterlander and was located at 3375 South Oakley Avenue. The rate commission assessed the value of the property based on a rent of $12,000, but the owner argued that this assessment was unfairly high because the property was in reality a detriment to him. It was haunted.

Denterlander was having a great deal of difficulty renting the property. A young woman had died there under mysterious circumstances - probably homicide - and since that time new tenants were grievously bothered by the sounds of moaning and crying. Tenant after tenant had walked out on their leases and it had become increasingly difficult to even attract renters.

140

The rate commission took the matter under advisement. After reviewing the case, it was decided to drop the assessment basis from $12,000 to $8,000 - a huge amount in 1912. The rate commission accepted the haunting of the building as factual, proving that even the taxman believes in ghosts!!

A GHOST ADOPTS A SON

One of the most spectacular cases which involved ghostly participation occurred in 1866 in England and was heard by the King's Bench, consisting of three justices. In this case, Mrs. Jane Lyon – a wealthy, aged widow – sued Daniel Home for the return of gifts she had given him, claiming he had used undue influence over her to get them. The influence he used was contact with the spirit of her dead husband, she said.

Daniel Home was a genuine spirit medium. He insisted on acting in total daylight and being tested with as many eyes observing him as possible. In full view, he levitated to the ceiling, raised hundredweight tables into the air, and levitated himself out one window and in through another window. He was not a fraud. According to him, he did not call upon the spirits, but they used him when THEY wanted to communicate. And he did not take pay for his services!

At an early meeting with Mrs. Lyon, Mr. Home received a message from her late husband, Charles. This started a long series of communications between medium and client. Eventually, the ghost of Charles requested that his wife, Jane, adopt Daniel Home as their son. She quickly agreed. And it was done. Daniel Home was legally adopted – legally – and became known as Daniel Lyon.

As the adopted son of the ghost and his wife, Daniel became heir to all of their fortune, and theirs was a considerable one. He also received many gifts, most in the form of money, from his "mother," Jane.

Eventually, Jane became wary of Daniel – through the intercession of a less than reliable female friend – and she went through a change of heart. She had become convinced that Daniel was swindling her, a charge which he vehemently denied.

But in 1866 Daniel Home was sued by his mother and it was claimed he had used undue influence over her to gain everything he had from her vast estate. Her argument was that because HE COULD AND DID contact the spirit of her dead husband he used this as power over her to obtain these possessions.

And the court of the King's Bench agreed. According to their findings, Daniel Home PROVED beyond legal doubt that he could and did contact spirits and that he used this special ability to unduly influence the elderly Mrs. Lyon. The outcome of the case is somewhat cloudy because the court also accused Mrs. Lyon of blatantly lying on the stand. Thus, while she won the case, she only received partial return of the possessions she gave to Mr. Home and she had to pay ALL court costs which is never done by the victor.

CLOSING STATEMENT

What to conclude from what has just been presented? What message is delivered by the courts of the world concerning the existence of ghosts and other paranormal phenomena?

The best way to answer is by reviewing the major decisions that have been rendered, keeping in mind that the court will not put forth as definitive a statement as: yes, ghosts do exist, or, no, they don't. Legal language does not sound like that. Legal decisions are implied. One of the most often used findings when considering something of a paranormal nature is that it was the result of unknown causes or an unidentified force or in one case, cosmic forces.

For clarity, the decisions of the Courts will be grouped by type, proceeding from cases dealing with financial advice and assistance to supernaturally revealed wills, then haunted houses, and then to the verdicts of the most serious nature, involving homicide. The cases involving homicide are of a critical nature because they profoundly affect people's lives and if a person is to be convicted on the evidence presented by a ghost and possibly be executed it must be assumed that the evidence is beyond a doubt because that is what is required in a murder trial. Is the ghostly evidence that strong?

Ghosts as providers of evidence have fared quite well in matters of financial advice, although in the courtroom proceedings that were examined the outcomes of the cases themselves were unrelated to the ghost's credibility. What does that mean? Basically that the existence of the ghost in the matter was accepted, but its advice was not deemed correct. For example, in Dean v. Ross the ghost is given the benefit of the doubt of having related some form of message to the medium, however, the jury did not believe that the pretend medium Mrs. Ross delivered the intended message.

In the matter of Burchill v. Hermameyer it is the court's opinion that while advice on where to look for oil may indeed have come from the spirit world the advice that the spirits gave was bad.

Concerning wills, ghosts fared quite well. In all instances examined they had - or would have had - a direct impact on the will in question, the outcome being that the will should be executed according to their, the ghosts,' intentions. The ghost of Thomas Harris saw his property divided equally between his four children which was the outcome that his ghost had come back to bring to pass. Major Blomberg's ghost returned on a foraging mission to reveal the hiding place of the tin box which held his will. But the ghost of Jasper Barker came back a little too late to effect the disposition of his will; thirty-three years too late. The statute of limitations had already run out by the time the ghost reappeared on earth. The judge even took him to task on his tardiness, saying that the ghost had no one else to blame but himself that his will had not been disposed of as he'd wanted. He should've made a timely appearance.

Ghosts made themselves quite believable in matters of haunted houses. Cases involving haunted houses are primarily matters of the breaking of leases due to dwellings deemed uninhabitable due to ghostly infestations. Such cases in which ghosts are found to be responsible for haunting houses and thus making them uninhabitable are not overly rare. The most famous is that of the 1991 Stombovsky v. Ackley case in Nyack, New York where the wording of the court's verdict was that the house was "legally haunted." The decision could not have been clearer. And what is it that haunts a house if not a ghost? This is as close as one can get to a legal statement saying - GHOSTS DO EXIST.

However, the indirect statements concerning ghosts in homicide cases are even more powerful. While a court's final ruling may be based on evidence obtained through the actions of a ghost, this will not be noted specifically in the written verdict, although the fact that the evidence was provided by a spirit will be declared in some manner, usually in the wording of the decision.

146

A prime example is the murder trial of C.T. Stewart, the man who was killed by a poison capsule given to him by his physician Dr. Lipscomb at the instigation of a man named Guy Jack. The court ruled that the statement the victim made about having come back from the dead to accuse his murderers was admissible NOT JUST AS A DEATHBED STATEMENT - because he was already dead when the statement was made - but as a statement of fact made by the spirit of the deceased. Part of the reason for accepting this statement as fact was that within it the ghost had revealed information that could not have been known by ordinary means - something supernatural had to have been involved. How else could the victim, Mr. Stewart, have known that Guy Jack had secretly taken out a life insurance policy on him? On this evidence Dr. Lipscomb was sentenced to be hung. He died in prison before the judgment could be carried out.

The ghost of Arline Stouts spoke to her father across her own grave and revealed who her murderer was. On this information Edwin King was arrested, tried and executed.

The ghost of Eric Tombe repeatedly appeared in his mother's dreams, informing her where he was buried and how he'd come to be murdered. On this information his body was discovered and his murderer, Earnest Dyer, committed suicide while the police were on route to arrest him.

Finally, is the case of Anne Walker. It is one of the most profound arguments in legal documents in favor of the existence of ghosts. Not only does it present two different sightings of an apparition but of two different ghosts, one of which was seen at the same time from different places in the courtroom by two different, highly credible witnesses.

Mr. Graime was visited at least three times by the ghost of Anne Walker, attempting to "convince" him to reveal her murderers. When he finally told the authorities what he knew, Mark Sharp and John Walker were brought to trial for the murder of Anne Walker and her unborn child. During the ensuing trial, the ghost of a young child appeared over the shoulder of Mr. Sharp and was seen by both the presiding judge and the jury foreman. Mark Sharp and John Walker were convicted of the crime and both were executed on the evidence brought to light by the ghost of Anne Walker.

Thus, in these most serious of crimes - homicide - the victim's ghosts actively sought justice and won it. But just because the courts relied upon evidence brought to light by ghosts does that mean that the courts believed in the ghosts themselves? This is the ULTIMATE QUESTION.

The answer is, yes - indirectly. The courts had to trace the trail of evidence back to its source, which in each instance was a ghost. The evidence could only be accepted as valid if the source was accepted and verified. This being so, the legal systems involved in the four murder cases just reviewed indirectly ruled that ghosts do exist otherwise the evidence that had been used to reach their verdicts could not have been ruled admissible. A court could not accept evidence from an imaginary entity!!!

Are ghosts real? Do they really exist? Now you be the judge.

The End

Have you seen a ghost?

www.ingramcontent.com/pod-product-compliance
Lightning Source LLC
Chambersburg PA
CBHW032145020426
42334CB00016B/1237